WELCOME TO

HORNEYTOWN
NORTH CAROLINA

POPULATION: 15

WELCOME TO

HORNEYTOWN

NORTH CAROLINA

POPULATION: 15

AN A TO Z TOUR THROUGH 201 OF THE
WORLD'S WEIRDEST & WILDEST PLACES

Quentin Parker

Avon, Massachusetts

Published by
Adams Media, a division of F+W Media, Inc.
57 Littlefield Street, Avon, MA 02322. U.S.A.
www.adamsmedia.com

ISBN 10: 1-4405-0454-7
ISBN 13: 978-1-4405-0454-9
eISBN 10: 1-4405-0739-2
eISBN 13: 978-1-4405-0739-7

Printed in the United States of America.

10 9 8 7 6 5 4 3 2 1

Library of Congress Cataloging-in-Publication Data
Parker, Quentin.
Welcome to Horneytown, North Carolina, population: 15 / Quentin Parker.
p. cm.
ISBN 978-1-4405-0454-9
1. City and town life—Humor. 2. Geography—Humor. I. Title.
PN6231.C455P37 2010
818'.602—dc22
2010009635

This publication is designed to provide accurate and authoritative information with regard to the subject matter covered. It is sold with the understanding that the publisher is not engaged in rendering legal, accounting, or other professional advice. If legal advice or other expert assistance is required, the services of a competent professional person should be sought.

—From a *Declaration of Principles* jointly adopted by a Committee of the
American Bar Association and a Committee of Publishers and Associations

Many of the designations used by manufacturers and sellers to distinguish their product are claimed as trademarks. Where those designations appear in this book and Adams Media was aware of a trademark claim, the designations have been printed with initial capital letters.

This book is available at quantity discounts for bulk purchases.
For information, please call 1-800-289-0963.

Dedication

To my wife, Tiffany, who is horrified at the thought of having this particular book dedicated to her.

ACKNOWLEDGMENTS

I would like to acknowledge Paula Munier for thinking a book about dirty place names would be a winner. I'd also like to thank all of those at Adams Media who have played any part in getting this book into its completed form. Finally, I'd like to thank my son, Parker, just because he's always an inspiration . . . even for a "dirty book."

 **WARNING**

Do not read this book if you reside in or near any of the following places:

Acock's Green, England
1

Aquinna (formerly Gay Head), Massachusetts
2

Arab, Alabama
3

Area 51, Rachel, Nevada
4

Bacchus, Utah
5

Bald Knob, Arkansas
6

Bangkok, Thailand
7

Bare, England
8

Bat Cave, North Carolina
9

Batman, Turkey
10

Battiest, Oklahoma
11

Beaver, Oklahoma
12

Beclean, Romania
13

Beedeville, Arkansas
14

Beer, England
15

Belchertown, Massachusetts
16

Big Bone Lick State Park, Kentucky
17

Big Ugly Creek, West Virginia
18

Bigadic, Turkey
19

Bird-in-Hand, Pennsylvania
20

Bitche, France
21

Bliss, Idaho
22

Blowing Rock, North Carolina
23

Blue Ball and Intercourse, Pennsylvania
24

Boca Raton, Florida
25

Boring, Oregon
26

Bowlegs, Oklahoma
27

Broadbottom, England
28

Brown Willy, England
29

Bugtussle, Kentucky
30

Bush, Kentucky
31

Busti, New York
32

Butternuts, New York
33

Buttzville, New Jersey
34

Catbrain, England
35

Christmas, Michigan
36

Climax and High Point,
North Carolina
37

Clowne, England
38

Cockburn, Australia
39

Cockermouth, England
40

Cockroach Bay, Florida
41

Come by Chance,
Australia
42

Conception, Missouri
43

Convict Lake,
California
44

Cowlic, Arizona
45

Coxsackie, New York
46

Crackpot, England
47

Crapo, Maryland
48

Crook, Colorado
49

Cumming, Georgia
50

Cunter, Switzerland
51

Cut and Shoot, Texas
52

Dead Horse Point
State Park, Utah
53

Dead Women Crossing,
Oklahoma
54

Devil's Dyke, England
55

Devil's Tramping
Ground, Siler City,
North Carolina
56

Dick Peaks, Antarctica
57

Dickshooter, Idaho
58

Dikshit, India
59

Dildo, Newfoundland
60

Ding Dong, Texas
61

Disappointment Creek,
Alaska
62

Disappointment
Islands, French
Polynesia
63

DISH, Texas
64

Diss, England
65

Dix, Nebraska
66

Dong, South Korea
67

Dumbell, Wyoming
68

Eclectic, Alabama
69

Eek, Alaska
70

Effin, Ireland
71

Eighty Four,
Pennsylvania
72

Enigma, Georgia
73

Euren, Wisconsin
74

Fagus, Missouri
75

Fifty-Six, Arkansas
76

Fingringhoe, England
77

Fishkill, New York
78

Flushing, Netherlands
79

The Fool Killer,
New Hampshire
80

Freak Lake, Alaska
81

French Lick, Indiana
82

Fucking, Austria
83

Fukuymama, Japan
84

Gay and Lesbian
Kingdom of the Coral
Sea Islands
85

Gay, Michigan
86

George, Washington
87

Glasscock County,
Texas
88

Gnaw Bone, Indiana
89

Gofuku, Japan
90

Great Snoring,
England
91

Gripe, Arizona
92

Gross, Nebraska
93

Happy, Texas
94

Hardwood, Oklahoma
95

Headless Chicken
Festival:
Fruita, Colorado
96

Head-Smashed-In
Buffalo Jump, Canada
97

Hell, Michigan
98

Hooker, Ohio
99

Hopeulikit, Georgia
100

Horneytown, North
Carolina
101

Hot Coffee, Mississippi
102

Hot Spot, Kentucky
103

Howlong, Australia
104

Humptulips,
Washington
105

Humpty Doo, Australia
106

Hungry Mother
State Park, Virginia
107

I.X.L., Oklahoma
108

Idiot Creek, Oregon
109

Inaccessible Island,
United Kingdom
Territory
110

Kaka, Arizona
111

Kill, Ireland
112

Kinki, Japan
113

Knob Lick, Missouri
114

Knockemstiff, Ohio
115

Lake Chargoggag-
oggmanchauggagog-
gchaubunagungam-
augg, Massachusetts
116

Lake Titicaca, Peru
and Bolivia
117

Layman, Ohio
118

Licking County, Ohio
119

Lizard Lick, North Carolina
120

The Lizzie Borden Bed and Breakfast, Fall River, Massachusetts
121

Llanfairpwllgwyngyllgogerychwyrndrobwllllantysiliogogogoch, Wales
122

Loco, Oklahoma
123

Looneyville, Texas
124

Lost, Scotland
125

Loveladies, New Jersey
126

Lower Ball's Falls, Canada
127

Maidenhead, England
128

Meat Camp, North Carolina
129

Mexican Hat, Utah
130

Mianus River, Connecticut
131

Middelfart, Denmark
132

Milk Shakes, Washington
133

Minge, Lithuania
134

Monkeys Eyebrow, Kentucky
135

Mono County, California
136

Monster, Holland
137

Morehead, Kentucky
138

Moron, Argentina
139

Mound, Louisiana
140

Mount Dick, New Zealand
141

Mount Faget, Antarctica
142

Mount Mee, Australia
143

Muckle Flugga, Scotland
144

Muff, Ireland
145

Mystery Spot, Santa Cruz, California
146

No Name, Colorado
147

Normal, Illinois
148

Nothing, Arizona
149

Odd, West Virginia
150

Oral, South Dakota
151

Peculiar, Missouri
152

Pee Pee, Ohio
153

Phuket, Thailand
154

Pippa Passes, Kentucky
155

Pussy, France
156

Raphoe, Ireland
157

Rock City, Tennessee
158

Sasmuan (formerly Sexmoan), Philippines
159

Shag Island, New Zealand
160

Shitterton, England
161

Show Low, Arizona
162

Silly, Belgium
163

Soddy-Daisy, Tennessee
164

South of the Border,
Dillon, South Carolina
165

Splott, Wales
166

Spread Eagle,
Wisconsin
167

Swastika, Ontario
168

Tarzan, Texas
169

Taumatawhakatangi-
hangakoauauota-
mateapokaiwhenuaki-
tanatahu Hill, New
Zealand
170

Te Puke, New Zealand
171

Tightsqueeze, Virginia
172

Tightwad, Missouri
173

Titz, Germany
174

Toad Suck, Arkansas
175

Tom, Dick, and
Harry Mountain,
Oregon
176

Tombstone, Arizona
177

Trim, Ireland
178

Truth or Consequences,
New Mexico
179

Turda, Romania
180

Twatt, Scotland
181

Two Egg, Florida
182

Ugley, England
183

Unalaska, Alaska
184

Vulcan, Canada
185

Wall Drug, South
Dakota
186

Wanker's Corner,
Oregon
187

Wee Waa, Australia
188

Weed, California
189

Wet Beaver
Wilderness, Arizona
190

Wetwang, England
191

What Cheer, Iowa
192

Whorehouse Meadow,
Oregon
193

Why, Arizona
194

Whynot, North
Carolina
195

Winchester
Mystery House,
California
196

Woody, California
197

Worms, Germany
198

Yaak, Montana
199

Zap, North Dakota
200

Zzyzx, California
201

INTRODUCTION

People travel and study the world to answer a plethora of challenging questions: What are other cultures like? Can global understanding lead to world peace? And, most critically: What countries have legal weed and prostitution?

But you've got just one question you want answered: Where can I, like, totally score some strange?

Fear not, noble—albeit horny—seeker of knowledge. Even a total loser like you can't help but score in Horneytown. And how could you miss in Intercourse or Dildo?

Well, okay, you might not be necessary in the last place, but you get the point.

The world is filled with places offering recreation, cultural opportunities, and names that are funny as shit.

With this book as a guide, you can find these places and even share important facts about them at your next drunken keg party. Because that guy next to you really is wondering what the population of Toad Suck, Arkansas is.

Some rudely named places can't help themselves. After all, it's not Thailand's fault that most of the world wants to call its resort city "fuck it" instead of "poo-ket." Or that the nearby Phi-Phi Islands are pronounced "pee pee" in English.

But WTF!? What *was* that horny bastard in Arizona thinking when he, um, came up with the name "Wet Beaver Wilderness" for an isolated spot? And why couldn't ancient tribes of Peru and Bolivia have figured out that "Titicaca" would someday make most people think of boobs and poop? Didn't those guys predict the world would end in 2012 or something? Oh, wait. That was the Mayans, but you get what I'm saying.

And while you're learning about the inadvertently weird, you might also find yourself wondering if places exist that are just, *de facto*, weird. Hell, yes!

How about an intergalactic truck stop in the desert of Nevada or the spot where the devil stalks—when he's not thinking of ways to torture you eternally for the sin of incessant masturbation—or a place made out of gazillions of bones? They're all here.

Now, go buy some condoms, cut your hair so your passport photo won't be so embarrassing, and get ready for me to take you to Horneytown.

ACOCK'S GREEN,
ENGLAND

Something terrible has happened! The constant masturbation, cheap hookers, and never changing your underwear have had some nasty effects on you. Acock's Green! Dude, don't get that freaking thing near me.

Acock's Green (sometimes written as *Acocks Green*, without the apostrophe) is, basically, a large area of Birmingham, England, adjacent to another suburb called Fox Hollies. Traffic in town can become pretty bad, apparently, but it does give people a chance to scrutinize all the green cocks in the community.

Acock's Green was named for a widespread syphilis epidemic that rocked this portion of Birmingham during Shakespeare's time. Just kidding! In fact, the community was named for the Acock family, which built a large home there in the fourteenth century.

Ever since, cheeky Brits and ugly, visiting Americans have laughed at the name of this community, which sounds like the symptom of some sort of horrible venereal disease that results in shriveled, putrid members. But then, you already know all about shriveled, putrid members. ↗

WHY IS YOUR ACOCK'S GREEN?

Acock's Green is a ward, or voting district, of south Birmingham.

WHY IS IT NAMED AFTER A SHRIVELED, PUTRID MEMBER?

Acock's Green actually was named for the Acock family, which built a large home in the area during the fourteenth century.

WHAT DO YOU NEED TO KNOW ABOUT ACOCK'S GREEN?

It has a skateboard park built with public funds, which locals hope will keep teens from becoming hooligans.

AQUINNA
(FORMERLY GAY HEAD),
MASSACHUSETTS

Rednecks are fond of saying that their devotion to the Confederacy's Stars and Bars is "heritage, not hate," even though anyone with more than one tooth and brain cell in his or her head realizes this is total bullshit. The fact that, in 1997, residents of Gay Head, Massachusetts changed the name of the town to Aquinna actually *does* reflect heritage and even an end to hate.

The Wampanoag tribe lived on the island formerly known as Gay Head. The best known Wampanoag is probably Squanto, who endured slavery by Spaniards yet *still* accepted the role of interpreter and general helpmate to British colonizers in the seventeenth century. The Wampanoags called part of their territory *Aquinna*, which means "land under the hill." White folks came in, took over, yadda yadda yadda. They decided to name the area *Gay Head* because they were gay and, hey, who doesn't like to get head?

In truth, it's not clear where *Gay Head* came from. Aquinna has many points, or heads, that dip out into the Atlantic Ocean, and *gay* used to only mean *happy*. So, you can do the math.

After being Gay Headers? Gay Headites? Gay Heads? For nearly 150 years, residents—many of whom are Wampanoags—voted to have their town revert to its original name. Don't be too upset, though. Aquinna may lack its Gay Head, but it still offers one of the few totally nude beaches along the eastern seaboard. ➚

WHERE CAN I GET SOME GAY HEAD?

You can't get it in the Martha's Vineyard community of Aquinna because it stopped being Gay Head in 1997.

WHY ISN'T IT GAY HEAD ANYMORE?

Locals, many of whom belong to the tribe that founded the community, voted to have the town revert to its original Wampanoag name. Of course, one also has to wonder if, in fact, people there were just sick of hearing jokes about giving "gay head."

WHAT DO YOU NEED TO KNOW ABOUT AQUINNA?

It has a nude beach. 'Nuff said.

ARAB,
ALABAMA

At a time when some Americans believe all Arabian people are terrorists bent on jihad, it's nice to know that there's one state where no one fears Arabs: Alabama. The folks in George Wallace's old state know that Arabs are simply small-town folks who are the salt of the earth.

Oh, wait. That's just people from the town of Arab. Most Alabamians actually hate Arabs who are from other countries. And, no, they're not aware that Arabs and Muslims are not the same thing. What do they care? They're from the same basic place, right?

Anyway . . . how did a little exurb of Birmingham come to be named for folks who practice jihad? Simple. The post office fucked up. Sounds typical.

It seems the town was *supposed* to be named *Arad*, as in Arad Thompson, son of the community's first postmaster. *Arad* isn't a hell of a lot better than *Arab*, mind you, but it beats the other names suggested for the fledgling town: Ink and Bird. Through a series of fuck ups, Arad became Arab, and the rest is history.

Nowadays, Arab is, ironically, 98 percent white. The other fine folks of Arab are listed as being from "other races." Could these elusive folks be the town's actual Arab population? ⟁

WHERE IS ARAB?

Arabs are found primarily in Saudi Arabia and Marshall County, Alabama.

WHY IS IT NAMED FOR ARABS?

It's not. The town was supposed to be named *Arad*, after a postmaster's son. The name got screwed up somewhere along the way.

WHAT DO YOU NEED TO KNOW ABOUT ARAB?

The idiots who founded the place not only couldn't get their name right, they also thought up stupid second choices such as Bird and Ink.

AREA 51,
RACHEL, NEVADA

Unless you're a Trekkie, or some other form of *Dwee-bus maximus,* you only have idle interest in UFOs. You have no trouble believing that there's no life in outer space. And you only watched the *X Files* because you thought Gillian Anderson or David Duchovny was hot.

Unfortunately, you share this planet with weirdos and fools who spend a good portion of their time trying to find evidence that we are not alone. The good news is these people never get laid, so their breed is certain to die out over time. Until this Utopia arrives, you'll have to hear about places like Area 51.

Located some eighty miles north of Las Vegas, Area 51 is, most likely, a place where the United States Air Force tests experimental planes and new weapons technology. Consequently, the U.S. government isn't inclined to make the goings-on at the base common knowledge.

Since Washington won't just tell us about these new death machines, conspiracy nuts have decided that the government is hiding something even more sinister than anti-matter rays and planes with payloads that can destroy entire continents. Yes, that's right. The government is hiding . . . E.T.! Weapons of mass destruction? Yawn. Green-skinned alien chicks? Hell, yes! Every night, folks flock to the area, many hefting a brew at Rachel, Nevada's Little A'Le'Inn, before heading out to take pictures of strange lights in the sky, hoping, apparently, for a taste of alien strange. Earth to dweebs: Get a freaking life. ↗

WHERE ARE THE NERDS FLOCKING?

Area 51 is in Southern Nevada, about eighty miles north of Las Vegas and smack fucking dab in the middle of nowhere.

WHY IS IT CALLED *AREA 51*?

Many theories abound; most of which are, as expected, bizarre. Many of the government-owned properties in the Southern Nevada desert are designated simply by numbers.

WHAT DO YOU NEED TO KNOW ABOUT AREA 51?

It's not LAX for aliens, dumb ass.

BACCHUS,
UTAH

Since you probably slept through English class or spent it nursing wicked hangovers, we will begin with a short explanation of why this particular town's name is funny . . . or at least weird as shit.

First, let's review literary terms. A *paradox* is a seemingly contradictory situation. Second, let's return to mythology. Bacchus was the Roman god of wine, ritual madness, and ecstasy. In modern parlance, he was the god of getting good and fucked up while being drunk as shit.

Utah is known for its predominantly Mormon population. Mormons are known for believing in weird things and for eschewing pretty much anything that has to do with Bacchus. Granted, Mormons once were notable for their belief in polygamy, and some renegade Mormons still try to practice this illegal activity, but Mormons manage to make threesomes, foursomes, and, uh, fivesomes about as sexy as a chunk of granite.

So, why is there a town named Bacchus in Utah? Was this someone's idea of a cosmic joke? How the hell else could it have happened? Naming a town in Utah Bacchus is like naming a stripper Mildred.

It turns out that the town has nothing to do with the Roman god of orgies and freak outs. In fact, it was named for T.E. Bacchus, superintendent of an explosives plant built in the community by the Hercules Power Company. Whew! Utah's reputation as the buzzkill capital of the world is safe! ↗

WHERE IS BACCHUS?
In Utah, of all places.

WHY IS IT NAMED AFTER THE ROMAN GOD OF ORGIES?
It's named for T.E. Bacchus, superintendent of an explosives factory built in the community.

WHAT DO YOU NEED TO KNOW ABOUT BACCHUS?
His Greek counterpart was Dionysus.

BALD KNOB,
ARKANSAS

Nope, this community was not named for shaved pubes, though it's an understandable error.

In fact, like some other locations in this book, this small Arkansas town is testament to a ridge, or small mountain, with no vegetation atop it. Folks in the South and in parts of the Midwest call these little mountains *knobs*.

Surely, someone must have thought to him or herself: "Some day, people will have increasingly juvenile senses of humor and, therefore, will find place names like 'Bald Knob' amusing and, therefore, might cause us to be the butt of ridicule."

If someone was brave enough to raise this issue, then his or her fellow townsfolk must have scoffed and said, "Nothing wrong with knobs." Dumb asses. The "bald knob" of the town's name is a low ridge that helped early travelers maneuver through the complete lack of anything interesting that one can find almost anywhere in Arkansas.

Bald Knob is located at the confluence of two of the state's natural wonders: the Ozarks and the Arkansas delta. Notable not only for scenic beauty, this region is also one of the most boring places to live in the entire world. It's true! Folks living in caves in Kabul have more interesting lives than the folks who call Bald Knob home. ↗

WHERE IS YOUR BALD KNOB?

Bald Knob is in White County, Arkansas, where the Ozark Mountains meet the Arkansas delta. You can get your own bald knob by going to a salon and requesting a complete *manscape*.

WHY DOES IT APPEAR TO BE NAMED FOR A PENIS?

In fact, Bald Knob is named for a small mountain, which has helped guide travelers for generations.

WHAT DO YOU NEED TO KNOW ABOUT BALD KNOB?

It appears to be named for a penis.

BANGKOK,
THAILAND

Those crazy Thai people . . . giving their cities names they know will attract English-speaking tourists. Don't they have any shame? Face it. Where would you rather go? Disneyworld, with its evocation of family fun, or Bangkok, which *actually* sounds like the happiest place on Earth?

The capital and largest city of Thailand gets its "bang" from the Thai word for a city along the banks of a river, and it gets its "kok" from its well-known sex-trade industry. Some might argue "kok" comes from the Thai name for a type of plum found in the region, but you know better.

You know what's really crazy? *Bangkok* is only one portion of the full name of the city, which is listed in the *Guinness Book of World Records* for having the world's longest (seems appropriate, right?) place name: *Krung Thep Mahanakhon Amon Rattanakosin Mahinthara Yuthaya Mahadilok Phop Noppharat Ratchathani Burirom Udomratchaniwet Mahasathan Amon Phiman Awatan Sathit Sakkathattiya Witsanukam Prasit.* Now, that's a lotta kok!

Translated, the name gives directions to several massage parlors. ⬈

WHERE CAN YOU BANGKOK?

At your mama's. Or, in Southern Thailand.

WHY BANGKOK?

Because it's so much fun. The name is a combination of words meaning something like "city on the river that has a whole bunch of Java plums in it."

WHAT ABOUT BANGKOK?

Its full name is the longest place name in the world. It has a population roughly the size of New York City. Most importantly, it sounds like slang for having sex.

BARE,
ENGLAND

And you thought the British were prudes. Nothing could be further from the truth. In fact, there's a community within Lancashire that Bares all. It's true! The place has Bare shops, Bare eateries, and even Bare nursing homes. Do you dare to bare?

Bare must be full of hardy souls because, though a seaside resort, it doesn't get the sort of nudity-welcoming temperatures that you might find, for example, in the South of France or in sunny California. Nonetheless, several thousand souls Bare themselves all year long. Hop on a plane, dude. Even *you* might get lucky in a place like this!

Oh, wait. Damn it! Turns out that *Bare* comes from the same stupid Anglo-Saxon word that causes another British town to be called *Beer* (see page 15) even though you won't find any more ale in its pubs than you'll find anywhere else. What a fucking rip off!

Bare comes from the word *bearu*, which means *grove*, as in trees. That's it? Trees? We were hoping for naked, glistening bodies and something other than that toad-belly-white flesh for which Brits are well-known.

Well, forget about it. You won't find naked hotties trotting about the shore, displaying muff (For Muff, see page 145). Of course, *you* could always travel to town and start a new trend. You know . . . drop trou, tell everyone you're "baring in Bare" or something like that. Hey, enjoy your time in gaol, and don't drop the soap! ↗

BARE WHERE?

Bare is a suburb of Morecambe, which is itself within the City of Lancaster district. Does this make sense? Shit, no! But it does to the Brits.

WHY IS IT NAMED AFTER NUDITY?

Bare is derived from the Anglo-Saxon word, *bearu*, which means *grove*.

WHAT DO YOU NEED TO KNOW ABOUT BARE?

You probably shouldn't really go there and drop your pants.

BAT CAVE,
NORTH CAROLINA

Holy underwear, Batman! You've been outed! No, we're not talking about your ambiguously gay relationship with your ward, Dick Grayson. We're talking about the secret location of your crime-fighting lab and home away from home: the Bat Cave. It's in the mountains of North Carolina. Who knew?

Bat Cave is a small town near Asheville that is named after a nearby cave containing elephants and Burmese pythons. Just kidding. It's filled with bats, moron. What else?

The cave itself is owned by a nature conservancy, and you can access it via a fairly challenging trail. Once there, you may see plenty of *guano* (a nice word for *bat shit*) or some beautiful wildflowers. Stick around long enough, and you may even see a cowled Bruce Wayne and his, um, "ward" emerge from the darkness in a totally rad souped-up Batmobile. Who knows? If you want to see that, all you've got to do is load up on shrooms prior to your hike. Happy hunting! ↗

HOLY GPS! WHERE IS THE BAT CAVE?

It's about forty-five miles from Asheville in Henderson County, North Carolina.

HOLY NEOLOGISM! WHY IS IT CALLED *BAT CAVE*?

Because it's near a cave filled with bats. Duh!

WHAT DO YOU NEED TO KNOW ABOUT BAT CAVE?

Store owners, bartenders, and residents in the community have heard every single motherfucking reference to Batman you possibly could imagine and would appreciate it if you would keep your goddamn mouth shut.

BATMAN,
TURKEY

Sometimes, shit happens in the world that you just can't make up. Case in point: Batman versus Batman. Holy Nolo contendere, Batman!

In 2008, the good people of the Turkish town of Batman attempted to sue *The Dark Knight* director, Christopher Nolan, for using the town's name without permission. *Wham! Biff! Oof!* WTF!?

First off, Batman has only been Batman since 1957. Prior to that, the Turkish town was called Iluh. Most likely, *Batman* is a contraction formed from the nearby Bati Raman Mountains.

The Bob Kane-created crime-fighting character has been frightening criminals since 1939. So, shouldn't such a lawsuit, at the very least, have sprung up in the 1960s, after that campy television show debuted?

Beyond the bizarre spectacle of having Batman suing Batman is the fact that Batman's mayor tried, somehow, to relate the success of *The Dark Knight* to several unsolved murders and to an alarming suicide rate among local women.

Shit, dude. Even The Riddler couldn't sort this one out. ↗

WHERE IS BATMAN?

Sometimes, he's in Bat Cave, North Carolina (see page 9). At other times, apparently, he serves as the provincial capital of Turkey's Batman Province.

WHY IS BATMAN *BATMAN*?

Most likely, *Batman* is short for "Bati Raman," the name of a local mountain chain.

WHAT DO YOU NEED TO KNOW ABOUT BATMAN?

His true identity is Bruce Wayne, numbnuts.

BATTIEST,
OKLAHOMA

Most folks, even most folks who live in the damn state, will say you'd have to be batty to live in Oklahoma. First off, the state has this completely arbitrary "panhandle" that makes the state look like, well, like a giant frying pan. Secondly, the state is neither part of the Midwest, West, Southwest, nor anything else. It's like a state without a region. Finally, *Oklahoma!* is the name of a cutesy musical that makes most people gag due to its cloying songs and plotline.

But one community in the state can claim— perhaps with pride, perhaps not—to be the battiest in the state. That community, of course, is *Battiest*. That's right. The name of the town is a synonym not just for crazy or mildly insane but for the craziest and the most insane. These folks aren't just batty freaks. They're the BATTIEST freaks, motherfucker.

The name of the town is not, it turns out, a direct reference to its residents, batty and freaky as they may be. Instead, it's a tribute to a Choctaw judge named Byington Battiest. Was *he* batty, or did he get his name because of a proficiency for catching or training bats? It's hard to say.

Nonetheless, the 250 or so fine folks of this McCurtain County community go on their batty way, acting crazy, causing scenes and ruckuses, and showing the United States—and the world beyond—what crazy REALLY means. ➚

WHERE'S THE BATTIEST SHIT GOING DOWN?

Battiest is in Oklahoma's McCurtain County, which is in the extreme southeast corner of the state.

WHY BATTIEST?

It's a tribute to a Choctaw judge who had that last name.

WHAT DO YOU NEED TO KNOW ABOUT BATTIEST?

These motherfuckers are CRAZY.

BEAVER,
OKLAHOMA

Why aren't the tourists pouring in? Not only is Beaver, Oklahoma, named after slang for a woman's private parts, but it also bills itself "The Cow Chip Capital of the World." Holy cow! What more could any world traveler possibly want?

During the third weekend of April, people from miles around (and even from international locations . . . no lie) converge on Beaver to claim top prize in the World Championship Cow Chip Throw (a copyrighted name!). The prize? A statue of a large beaver holding a large cow turd! Start warming up that pitchin' arm right now!

When this Oklahoma-panhandle community first began, it was called *Beaver City*, which seems like a pretty good advertisement for horny fur trappers. Over time, the city morphed simply into *Beaver*, named for the Beaver River, which attracted large numbers of pelt traders during the nineteenth century.

Just remember . . . if you're ever lucky enough to find yourself in Beaver, make sure you pick up a shellacked cow chip as a souvenir to take home. Heck, buy one for all of your friends (or enemies)! ↗

> **I'M WORRIED ABOUT THE BEAVER. I CAN'T FIND HIM.**
>
> Beaver, Oklahoma is in the easternmost of the state's three panhandle counties.

> **WHERE IS MY BEAVER?**
>
> You can find it on about half of the human race.

> **WHAT DO I NEED TO KNOW ABOUT BEAVER?**
>
> It's slippery when wet. Oh, and since 1970, it has been home to the annual World Championship Cow Chip Throw.

BECLEAN,
ROMANIA

There's a town in Romania that is just waiting to wash your mouth out with soap. They do not condone oaths or even mild curses. You watch yourself! These folks want you to Beclean.

Or, perhaps, there's a town in Romania in which everyone is obsessed with cleanliness. After all, isn't it supposed to be next to godliness? The fresh-smelling folks of this Transylvanian village want you to Beclean.

Or, wait a minute, maybe the folks of Beclean have this name because they often forget to take baths and showers. These stinky people who live in a part of the world associated mostly with Dracula or Vlad the Impaler constantly have to remind themselves to Beclean.

Actually, *Beclean* is an English approximation of the town's Hungarian and German name: *Bethlen*. *Bethlen* is a family name that has existed for centuries in Romania, and this town was once covered in Bethlens.

In addition to having a name that reminds people not to be potty mouths or dirty butts, Beclean is known in Romania for having an important railway junction that connects a bunch of communities that have names with *way* too many consonants and vowels for their own goddamn good: Sighetu Marmatiei and Suceava among them. ↗

> **WHERE CAN I BECLEAN?**
> Beclean is in the Transylvanian region of Romania.

> **WHY IS IT NAMED BECLEAN?**
> The name is an English approximation of *Bethlen*, a family associated with the community.

> **WHAT DO YOU NEED TO KNOW ABOUT BECLEAN?**
> If you go, please take a bath and keep your filthy-ass mouth shut!

BEEDEVILLE,
ARKANSAS

Feeling troubled? Sleepless nights? Hazy days? In short: Is something bedeviling you? Then we've found the perfect spot, a place you can go to exorcise those demons. The only drawback? It's in Arkansas, home to nothing but toothless mutant mouth-breathers and presidents who can't keep their peckers in their pockets.

If the entire state of Arkansas is the middle of nowhere, then Beedeville is in the armpit of the middle of nowhere. Perhaps that's why the folks there are so bedeviled in the first place. They're miserable and in want of lives. Still, you might as well visit and meet the devil face to face.

At first glance, it appears that the fine folks of Beedeville (population 105!) do not have a clue how to spell. Or maybe they're French and want to add extra "e's" and "l's" in places where they clearly do not belong. But, no! They may be mutant mouth-breathers, but they're not completely stupid.

Beedeville is named for the town's founding family: the Beedes. So, you see, the name of the town is not pronounced like *bedevil*. It's pronounced *bead-ville*. No jury would convict you, however, if you were to mispronounce the name of this municipality, claiming in your defense that it is Hell on Earth.

Besides, you'd be wrong. If you're looking for Hell, you have to visit Michigan (see page 98). ↗

WHERE THE BEDEVIL IS BEEDEVILLE?

It's in Jackson County, Arkansas, putting it right smack dab in the middle of freaking nowhere.

HOW DID IT BECOME *BEEDEVILLE*?

The town's name is pronounced *Beadville* because it was founded by folks named *Beede*. A settler's descendant is the current mayor, but, then again, who gives a shit?

WHAT DO YOU NEED TO KNOW ABOUT BEEDEVILLE?

There's just not a whole hell of a lot to know.

BEER,
ENGLAND

Now, this is our kind of place! An entire town devoted to the greatest beverage ever invented by mankind. Picture folks riding boats in Beer ponds! Cars that run on Budweiser or Yardley's Stout or whatever the fuck kind of beer it is folks drink in England. Grocery stores that sell nothing but beer! Optometrists that sell only Beer goggles! Wow. The mind reels.

Wait a minute! This town's not named for the stuff you drink in your parents' basement, alone, every weekend. *Beer* is derived from an Anglo-Saxon word, *bearu*, which means *grove*. Once upon a time, Beer was heavily forested.

Even though the town isn't really named for beer, it's still worth a visit. The town grew up around caves once used by pirates and smugglers, and the seaside village contains many bucolic sites, including Beer Head.

Beer Head is *not* named for the only kind of sex you've ever received. In fact, it is a picturesque cliff that helps protect Beer from vicious western winds. Still, wouldn't you love to be able to talk about "Beer Head" in mixed company, you know, like to your grandma or something?

So, raise a glass to the fine people of Beer, home to frothy liquids, public urination, and Beer Head. Good times. Good times. ↗

WHERE CAN I GET SOME BEER?

It's a village in County Devon, at the southern tip of England.

WHY IS IT NAMED FOR BEER?

It isn't. *Beer* derives from an Anglo-Saxon word that means *grove*.

WHAT DO YOU NEED TO KNOW ABOUT BEER?

You're almost out, but don't come around trying to borrow any of ours, asshole.

BELCHERTOWN,
MASSACHUSETTS

What's worse? A town that sounds like it was named for a mouth fart or the fact that the town was, in fact, named for a traitor . . . a royal governor who probably would have been more than happy to boil Paul Revere—and his horse—in oil and serve it with spotted dicks and beans or whatever the fuck it is Brits eat?

Belchertown is named for Jonathan Belcher, Massachusetts's royal governor from 1730 to 1741. His family name arose because these folks farted and belched more loudly, and with more gusto, than any other family in the Motherland. Okay, that's not true. The family just happened to have a funny name. You know how it is. At least they weren't named, like, the Shitters or something.

Belchertown gained a nanosecond of fame in the early days of George W. Bush's presidency. Calls for those seeking employment in the administration were routed through Belchertown, despite the fact that only sixteen percent of the city's residents are registered Republicans.

Calls to the Belchertown number spent about a nanosecond—roughly the length of time Dick Cheney gave Bush to run the country during the eight-year co-presidency—in town before being routed to Washington. ↗

WHERE (BELCH) IS IT?

Belchertown is about fifteen miles from Amherst, best known as the home to famous recluse and poster child for demented poets, Emily Dickinson.

WHY (BURP) IS IT NAMED BELCHERTOWN?

The town is named for Jonathan Belcher, a Tory governor for the Massachusetts colony from 1730 to 1741.

WHAT (BELCH, BURP) DO I NEED TO KNOW ABOUT BELCHERTOWN?

Belchertown once had a shameful association with that guy who was president before Barack Obama. What was his name? Oh yeah. Dick Cheney.

BIG BONE LICK STATE PARK,
KENTUCKY

Imagine being the poor schmuck who has to answer the phone this way: "Big Bone Lick. Can I help you?" He probably hates his life. He probably hates you. He especially hates mammoths.

Why mammoths? They helped to give this Kentucky state park its name. During the Pleistocene era, mammoths and other creatures that weren't fat—they were big-boned—came to the area for its natural salt lick. Some died nearby. *Voila*! Big Bone Lick.

William Clark, of Lewis and Clark fame, was the first to pick up a mammoth remain and stroke his big bone. Thus, the park declares itself "The Birthplace of American Paleontology." Wow! That one must excite the kids.

In 2009, Big Bone Lick State Park was named a National Natural Landmark. In an effort to attract more female tourists, the park has considered changing its name to Mammoth Freakin' Bone Lick State Park. ↗

WHERE CAN I GET A BIG BONE?

In your pants, if you've been gifted by God. Otherwise, it's in Boone County, Kentucky.

HOW DID YOUR BIG BONE GET ITS NAME?

Well, one thing's for sure. It wasn't your girlfriend. The zany combination of a salt lick and giant Pleistocene-era animal bones led to what is surely the greatest of all state park names.

WHAT DO YOU NEED TO KNOW ABOUT BIG BONE?

It's a National Natural Landmark. It's the site of what may well have been America's first archeological dig. It's something you will never, never have.

BIG UGLY CREEK,
WEST VIRGINIA

If years of living together have turned your once-hot babe into someone you can only touch while wearing beer goggles, then here's the perfect way to send her a subtle message: Plan a vacation along West Virginia's Big Ugly Creek.

Some argue the creek owes its name to railroad surveyors whose jobs were made difficult because the area is rugged and full of brush. Others say the creek got its name because the land around it isn't good for farming. Still others claim it was named for your mama, biatch.

Big Ugly Creek is some twenty miles long, and it's a major tributary of West Virginia's Guyandotte River. If you're ever in the region, be sure to visit the nearby town of Big Ugly and say "hi" to your mama for me. ⬈

WHERE IS THIS BIG UGLY PLACE?

Wherever your girl-friend lives. Oh, wait. *That's* Butt Ugly. Big Ugly is in Lincoln County, West Virginia.

WHY YOU SO BIG AND UGLY?

Railroad surveyors with bad attitudes. Failed farmers with bad attitudes. Your mom once visited the area.

YOUR MAMA SAY YOU BIG UGLY

Big Ugly Creek is a tributary of the Guy-andotte River. It's roughly twenty miles long. I'll resist ending with yet another your-mama joke.

BIGADIC,
TURKEY

Dang, the men in this Turkish town must love to visit English-speaking countries. *Yeah, baby. That's right. I'm from Bigadic. I keep proof in my pants. Would you like to see?* Unfortunately for any excited young women, *Bigadic* does not have any connection to the English words *big dick*. Sorry, ladies!

Theories abound concerning the etymology of this small town in Balekisir Province. Some claim that it descends from the name of a Roman general. Some believe it is a modernization of an ancient place name that meant "twin of the goddess of luck." And some claim the name actually *should* be *Bogadic*, which means "meadow for bulls."

But if the men in town are smart, they'll move to revise history. They'll claim that the town is, in fact, named for bulls . . . but only for their balls. I mean, *damn*, have you seen those things? They hang down like four feet!

So, the next time a Turkish swinger meets a young English-speaking lady, he should tell her, "Oh, Bigadic does not have anything to do with a big dick, but it's got everything to do with big balls. Of course," he will add, "in *my* case, it *does* also stand for 'big dick.' Would you like to see?" Good luck, bro. ⟿

WHERE CAN I GET BIGADIC?

If you're extremely lucky—and most likely, you are not so blessed—then you'll find it in your pants. Otherwise, you'll have to check out the Balekisir Province of Turkey.

HOW DID IT GET TO BE NAMED FOR A BIG DICK?

Depending on whom you ask, the town is actually named for: A. a Roman general; B. a goddess of luck; or C. a meadow for bulls.

WHAT DO YOU NEED TO KNOW ABOUT BIGADIC?

It has natural hot mineral springs, which it's said give residents big dicks.

BIRD-IN-HAND,
PENNSYLVANIA

Okay, so let's get this straight. The Pennsylvania Dutch country, full of Amish folks and shoo-fly pie and down-home values is home to towns celebrating sex (Intercourse, see page 24), a lack of sex (Blue Ball, see page 24), and even masturbation. And you thought evangelicals had a lock on fucked up shit!

Bird-in-Hand, the aforementioned bastion of masturbation, is in Lancaster County, not far from Intercourse. Apparently, if you can't find Intercourse and you don't want to endure Blue Ball(s), you can settle for the third path: Bird-in-Hand. Just grab that bird and start strokin'.

The community dates back to the eighteenth century, and so does its name. Once, long ago, the village was dominated by an inn called Bird-in-Hand that featured the aforementioned bird and hand on its sign. Most likely, this was, literally, a bird and not a penis being stroked by a disembodied hand. But who knows? The sign has been gone for a very long time.

When you're not involved with your own bird-in-hand, you can take advantage of the exciting sites in this part of Amish country. There are . . . Amish farm tours! Amish country homesteads! And even the Amish Experience Theatre. Wait a minute . . . how can they have a theatre?

Oh well. You know what? On second thought, we'd rather just take that bird-in-hand and jerk off to pass the time . . . at least until we arrive in Intercourse. ➐

> **WHERE IS BIRD-IN-HAND?**
>
> It's in the Pennsylvania Dutch country, not far from Intercourse.

> **WHY IS IT NAMED FOR JERKING OFF?**
>
> Bird-in-Hand got its name from an old sign that featured a bird and a hand.

> **WHAT DO YOU NEED TO KNOW ABOUT BIRD-IN-HAND?**
>
> It is filled with the same kinky Amish people who brought you Intercourse and Blue Ball. And too much will make you go blind.

BITCHE,
FRANCE

Bienvenue a Bitche, or, "Welcome to Bitche," crows the website for this beautiful rural town near the German border. Just watch yourself while you're there enjoying Bitche's forests, golf, lakes, and ancient fortress. Get out of line, and the local *policier* have orders to Bitche slap you, motherfucker.

Bitche is dominated by a large rock, which has been the home of citadels and fortresses (is there a difference?) since time immemorial. Early references to the fortress called it *Bytis Castrum,* which sounds kind of like "castrating bitch" but basically means "fortified place." So, there you go. That's how a town full of Bitches winds up in some of the prettiest countryside in France.

These Bitches tried to protect themselves after World War I by making their fortress part of the Maginot Line, basically a series of obstacles, embankments, fortresses, and machine gun posts that ran along France's borders with Germany and Italy.

But, as we all know, the Germans and Italians laughed at these Bitches and took over the country anyway, making France—to this day—synonymous with cowardice in battle. Take that, Bitches! ↗

WASSUP, BITCHE?
Bitche is a lovely little town in northern France, near the German border.

MAN, DON'T BE A BITCHE.
Bitche is a modernized French version of Latin words that mean "fortified place." It is dominated by a large rock that has long been the site of a fortress.

TAKE THAT, BITCHE!
The area around the town is called *Pays de Bitche*, which basically means "Bitche Country."

BLISS,
IDAHO

Are you looking for a state of extreme happiness? Nirvana on Earth? Complete ecstasy at every waking moment? The opportunity to live in the middle of fucking nowhere in a state best known for potatoes and not much else? Well, then, son. Head for Bliss.

Bliss, Idaho was named for settler David B. Bliss. In other words, this Podunk town of 275 was not named for anything truly blissful. Perhaps Mr. Bliss figured that, if the town bore his name, folks would flock to this tiny corner of Idaho's Gooding County.

Alas, it didn't seem to work. Bliss remains a small, small town more than a half-mile above sea level. While there, you can . . . sit on your ass. Or twiddle your thumbs. Or count ceiling tiles. The opportunities are endless (if you have no freaking life nor ever aspire to one)!

Actually, come to think of it, Eastern religions might define *bliss* as "action through inaction." You know, all that Zen bullshit about focusing on the inner life and not on outward stuff like owning Hummers (or getting a hummer in the backseat of your Hummer).

If that's truly bliss, then Bliss might be the place to find bliss after all. While you twiddle your thumbs or masturbate for the thirteenth time on that particular day, perhaps your inner mind will become at one with the universe.

Nah. You might as well just start yanking your crank again. ⬈

WHERE CAN I FIND ETERNAL BLISS?

Probably not in the middle of Idaho. But you can find a community called Bliss in the potato state's Gooding County.

IS IT REALLY SO *BLISSFUL*?

Who knows? The town was named for an early settler, whose last name was Bliss.

WHAT IS THERE TO KNOW OF BLISS?

It is a state best attained when one is not seeking it, grasshopper. So a place with nothing to do might actually be the perfect place to seek bliss.

BLOWING ROCK,
NORTH CAROLINA

Man, you've got to have the beer goggles to end all beer goggles in order to scam on a rock, much less to blow it. Yet, there is a community in North Carolina that possesses these amazing beer goggles. Folks in those parts are more than willing to try Blowing Rock.

What is it like? Is it hard? Is it cold? On which outcropping do most folks affix their orifices? Does anything, you know, come out of the outcropping when the blowing is done? So many questions . . . and so few answers. You may have to go and try Blowing Rock yourself.

With the exception of the presence of freaks with bizarre sexual habits, Blowing Rock is a beautiful community nestled in the mountains of Caldwell and Watauga counties. Allegedly, the name of the town comes from an unusual geological formation above the Johns River Gorge.

If you stand on a particular cliff over the gorge and drop something, the strong updraft from the gorge is said to blow the item back up to you. Try it first on, say, a small child before you jump off the cliff yourself.

Or just choose a little safe sex and try Blowing Rock for yourself. ↗

WHERE IS BLOWING ROCK?

Blowing Rock, North Carolina can be found in two counties: Caldwell and Watauga. The actual blowing rock is near the eponymous town.

WHY IS IT NAMED FOR SEXUAL PRACTICES INVOLVING ROCKS?

Blowing Rock is named for a geological formation that causes high winds to blow up from a gorge.

WHAT DO YOU NEED TO KNOW ABOUT BLOWING ROCK?

Rocks prefer you to spit, not swallow.

BLUE BALL AND INTERCOURSE,
PENNSYLVANIA

The Pennsylvania Dutch Amish are known for rejecting technology, for driving around in buggies, for sporting cool facial hair (the men, primarily), and for creating arts and crafts. Who knew they were also kinky freaks?

It's true! These two Amish country towns are a stone's throw from one another in the lower southeastern corner of Pennsylvania: Intercourse and Blue Ball.

As anyone who has been, or currently is, a horny teenage boy knows, *blue balls* is a painful affliction resulting from not, um, relieving erections older men chew on Cialis to acquire. Blue Ball, on the other hand, is a community named for the Blue Ball Inn, which stood in the area for more than 200 years.

Intercourse is, perhaps, the most pleasurable way to avoid blue balls. It is also the name of a town so-called for reasons lost to history. Some suggest the community is named for a horse track, Entercourse, which once stood nearby. Others believe the name was adopted because, though it has sexual connotations, it also suggests social interaction and harmony. Still others believe the name was adopted because the original town name, *Fucking*, was already taken by a spot in Austria (See page 83). ↗

WHERE CAN I FIND KINKY AMISH SEX?

Intercourse and Blue Ball are unincorporated villages in Pennsylvania's Lancaster County.

HOW DID INTERCOURSE AND BLUE BALL COME TO BE?

Well, when two people love each other very much . . . okay, okay. *Intercourse* might have been named for a race track, or it might refer to the nonsexual meanings of *intercourse*. Blue Ball is named for the Blue Ball Inn.

WHAT DO I NEED TO KNOW ABOUT INTERCOURSE AND BLUE BALL?

They are charming communities. They are filled with the Amish. Intercourse counteracts Blue Balls.

BOCA RATON,
FLORIDA

Thank God you're a typical American whose Spanish vocabulary extends solely to whatever you get from Taco Bell before you puke it up early Sunday morning. Otherwise, you'd think twice about that trip you're planning to Boca Raton. It's not just that the women there are no more interested in you than the ones with big hair that you see at the mall. In addition, just what kind of skank do you expect to pick up in a town that's Spanish for "rat's mouth"?

It's true! In Spanish, *boca* means "mouth." Boca Raton sits on a small inlet, and Spanish explorers often called these small inlets *mouths*. And *rata* means "rat." Explorers called rocks that liked to "gnaw" on ship's cables *ratas* or *ratons*.

Some folks like to believe that the town's name actually refers to the fact that, at one time, Boca Raton was a pirate stronghold. The name of the community refers to the rats, or scoundrels, chasing booty in the area. You know, just like you're hoping to do.

Nowadays, Boca Raton is one of those coastal communities in which houses cost more than the gross domestic product of many third-world countries. Everyone who lives there must take an oath of loyalty to Ronald Reagan and must never, ever utter the words "socialized medicine," though the words "social security" are okay.

Not bad for a place named after a rat's orifice. ↗

WHERE CAN I FIND RAT'S MOUTH?

Boca Raton is in Palm Beach County, not far from Miami.

WHY IS IT NAMED RAT'S MOUTH?

Boca means "mouth." Spanish explorers called small inlets mouths. They named rocks that liked to chew up ship's ropes *raton*, or *rat/mouse*.

WHAT DO YOU NEED TO KNOW ABOUT RAT'S MOUTH?

The city does not actually demand fealty to Ronald Reagan. Just to Satan.

BORING,
OREGON

Folks in Boring are proud to be, well, Boring. Their town is filled with Boring businesses selling Boring items and Boring families having Boring sex and producing Boring children. The community bills itself "the most exciting place to live" (no lie). So, with all of the millions of boring places that exist on this planet, how did one small town in Oregon get to be the, um, champion of boredom?

Boring is named for an early settler who had this unfortunate last name. Why the townspeople thought that naming the community after this guy made sense is anybody's guess. But, then again, we're talking about Oregon here. Remember the Jail Blazers? A team full of sex offenders and drug addicts who nearly bankrupted an NBA franchise that, at one point, had been among the most popular in the nation? Genius is not this state's strong suit.

While in Boring, you can see all kinds of Boring sites. Try the Boring water fountain, the Boring town square, or attend services at the Assembly of God in Boring (no lie) where Boring pastors will attempt to save your Boring soul. Hallelujah!

You might even want to attend the Boring Lava Field. It's true! A field of extinct, 2.5 million-year-old volcanoes was named for nearby Boring. You could call this truth in advertising. Some 300,000 years ago you would have seen all kinds of action. Nowadays, you look at . . . a bunch of extinct volcanoes just sitting there being Boring. Good times. Good times. ↗

COULD YOU BE MORE BORING?

Boring is in Oregon's Clackamas County, not far from slightly-less-boring Portland.

GOD, YOU'RE BORING.

That's what people probably said to W.H. Boring, an early settler for whom the unincorporated community was named.

WHAT DO YOU NEED TO KNOW ABOUT BORING?

It's near some extinct (yawn) volcanoes. It bills itself "the most exciting place to live." Somehow, I doubt that.

BOWLEGS,
OKLAHOMA

Holy shit! As hard as it may be to believe, there are folks in an Oklahoma community who argue over whom to thank (to blame?) for naming the town *Bowlegs*.

First off, we'd like to make one thing clear: The town is *not* named for the medical condition, *Genu varum*, which causes a person's thighs to bend out like bows, making one a laughingstock in school and a constant visitor in later years to a therapist's couch.

No. The town is named for Billy Bowlegs, a Seminole chief. This man would not give up the good fight. He was a leader of the Second and Third Seminole Wars with the United States. Ultimately, Bowlegs was defeated, and he "retired" to Indian Territory — later to become the state of Oklahoma.

Or is it? Others contend that, instead, "Bowlegs" (the community) is named for Lula Bowlegs, a descendant of Billy Bowlegs who settled in the area.

One is left with only one question: Who the fuck cares? Your community sounds like it was named for someone who walks funny, someone who resembles a rubbery cartoon figure brought to life! What's the matter with you? What you *really* should be concerned about is changing your name to something more pleasant, like Seminole (oops, sorry, there's already one of those in your county), Bolek (a variation of Billy Bowlegs's name), or, for Chrissakes . . . Flowerpot. Something that doesn't sound like *bowlegs*. Wake up, Oklahoma! ➚

▶ WHERE IS BOWLEGS?

Bowlegs is in Seminole County, Oklahoma, just about in the center of the state.

▶ WHY IS IT NAMED BOWLEGS?

The town probably was named for a Seminole Chief, Billy Bowlegs, whose walk was perfectly normal, thank you very much.

▶ WHAT DO YOU NEED TO KNOW ABOUT BOWLEGS?

The condition's scientific name is *Genu varum*.

BROADBOTTOM,
ENGLAND

If you are a chubby chaser—and you probably are, you kinky freak, you—then there's a village in England you've just gotta see! Folks in the town are proud of being fat asses. They chose, however, to be a bit discreet. So, rather than being the town of *Fatass*, they became the town of *Broadbottom*.

Broadbottom is a village within Manchester. Everything in town is made to accommodate the villagers' fat asses: extra wide seats at the pub, the movie theater, and even the loo (the funny British name for *bathroom*) . . . perfect for folks like Idaho senator Larry Craig and his infamous "widened stance."

Okay, okay. Everything in the previous paragraph—with the exception of Larry Craig's widened stance and the location of the town—is pure fiction. The village of Broadbottom takes its name from fourteenth-century landowner William de Brodebothum who once lived in town. Of course, the question still remains: Why the fuck, when the village decided to "modernize" Brodebothum's name, did town leaders choose a new name that's a synonym for *fat ass*?

Did they *really* want their daughters to be called *Broadbottom lasses*? Did they want to pig out at Broadbottom restaurants? And, whilst quaffing Bass Ale, did they want to consider the results of imbibing *too* many empty calories at Broadbottom pubs? What the hell is the *matter* with you, Broadbottom people? Go on a diet, already, so you can change the name of your town to *Slenderbottom* or *Skinny Ass*. ↗

WHERE'S YOUR BROADBOTTOM?

It's inside your size XXL pants, fat ass.

WHY IS IT NAMED FOR FAT ASSES?

Broadbottom is derived from the name of an early area landowner, William de Brodebothum.

WHAT DO YOU NEED TO KNOW ABOUT BROADBOTTOM?

The people in town are fucking sick of fat-ass jokes, so keep them to yourself.

BROWN WILLY,
ENGLAND

Now it can be told! The highest point in England's County Cornwall—which, come to think of it, looks like a penis jutting out from England's southern tip—is named after a schlong!

That's right. You can go traipse among the moors like the brooding Heathcliff himself, until you come to that massive, round hill, which veritably ejaculates 1,000 feet from the countryside. Then it's, "Hallllooo, Brown Willy, so glad you could come."

Brown Willy is a laughably Anglicized form of the Cornish, *Bron Wennyly*, which means "swallows' hill." So, "large brown penis" and "swallow" come together on this Cornish landmark.

Something else that locals find hard to swallow is the so-called Brown-Willy Effect. The hill basically concentrates moisture in the atmosphere, causing massive showers to arise and drench areas to the north. Sometimes, he can't control himself and floods surrounding areas. Yep, that's right. It's as though Brown Willy is ejaculating all over southern England. ↗

OH WHERE, OH WHERE CAN MY BROWN WILLY BE?

Brown Willy is a 1,000-foot hill in Cornwall, England's southernmost county.

OH WHERE, OH WHERE CAN HE BE?

Brown Willy is bastardized English for *Bron Wennyly*, Cornish for *swallows' hill*.

WHAT DO YOU NEED TO KNOW ABOUT BROWN WILLY?

The hill, though no fault of its own, appears to be named after a brown penis.

BUGTUSSLE,
KENTUCKY

It's not often you find a town with an intentionally funny name. Frankly, most of the funny names in this book have logical explanations: derivations of American Indian words, Anglicization of Celtic words, tributes to people with unintentionally funny names, etc.

But Bugtussle is *Bugtussle* on purpose. Sharp-eyed fans of *The Beverly Hillbillies* may recognize the name as that of the Clampett's fictional hometown, but the show was just borrowing the actual name of an actual town. Shit . . . to be fair to Kentucky Bugtusslians (?), there are at least *four* Bugtussles in the United States (the others are in Alabama, Texas, and Oklahoma).

The one in Kentucky can be found in Monroe County. How did it get its name? Local comedians in this small community got so sick of fighting the local doodlebug population that they came to call their town *Bugtussle*, as in, fighting with bugs.

Now, if you're like me, you probably thought doodlebugs were fictional creatures. But no! *Doodlebugs*, also known as *pill bugs* or *roly polies*, belong to the wood lice family. They can wreak havoc on buildings.

Apparently, folks in this community had homes that were under constant attack, so they came up with a brilliant plan: they all decided to live in trailer parks. ↗

WHERE IS BUGTUSSLE?

Bugtussle can be found in four different states, including Kentucky. The Kentucky town is found in Monroe County.

WHY IS IT NAMED BUGTUSSLE?

A wood lice, or doodlebug, infestation led local wags to christen their town *Bugtussle* because of the constant bug battle.

WHAT DO YOU NEED TO KNOW ABOUT BUGTUSSLE?

It is the hometown of the Clampett family, who loaded up their truck and moved to Beverly. Hills, that is.

BUSH,
KENTUCKY

Who knew? The place even *you* can be sure to find some Bush is in the coal region of Kentucky. Yep . . . thirty-seven square miles of Bush. Bush everywhere. Of course, if you're not into Bush, you might have to consider visiting Brazilian Wax, Oregon or Shaved, Idaho. (Note: The latter two cities do not exist . . . as far as I know.)

Bush was named after George Bush. It's true! Of course, is this really a surprise since Kentucky, traditionally, has been a Red State? It does seem odd, though, that the community named itself after two guys who wouldn't be president for, like, a hundred years or so. It's like this part of Kentucky has second-sight or something . . . .

Oh, wait. *This* George Bush was just a storekeeper who was among the first to settle in the region. I wonder if he was an asshole, too? After all, he decided to name the town after himself. Or did he? Maybe he really just liked bush and thought it would be a giggle to give his town a permanent double entendre.

But that's pretty unlikely. Do folks in Kentucky even know what a *double entendre* is? Isn't that, like, French or something? One way or another, this little town in the heart of Kentucky coal country is *the* spot to find Bush in America. ↗

WHERE IS BUSH?

Well, you don't really see it much anymore, since the shaved look emerged sometime around the turn of the twenty-first century.

WHY BUSH?

Stupid question. Oh, it was named for George Bush, shopkeeper, not cringe-inducing president.

WHAT DO YOU NEED TO KNOW ABOUT BUSH?

It appears to be named after a slang word for *vagina*.

BUSTI,
NEW YORK

I must, I must, I must increase my bust! Bazoombas. Bee-stings. Cans. Dairy pillows. Gazongas. Headlights. Honkers. Hooters. Melons. Torpedoes. You'll find all varieties in Busti, New York!

Don't be a boob. The place isn't really named for funbags, speed bumps, juggs, or ta ta's. Busti is named for Paolo Busti, principal agent of the Holland Land Company from 1800 to 1824. The Holland Land Company once owned a whopping gazonga-sized portion of western New York.

Nowadays, Busti is a quiet little town in New York's Chautauqua County, containing roughly 8,000 man boobs and about 8,000 goombas, hood ornaments, mounds, nose warmers, and sweater cows. ➹

WHERE IS HONKERS . . . ER, BUSTI, NEW YORK?

Busti is in New York's Chautauqua County.

WHY IS IT NAMED AFTER BREASTS?

It isn't. It's named for Paolo Busti, an official with the Holland Land Company. History does not leave us the answer to the burning question: Did Busti have man boobs?

WHAT DO I NEED TO KNOW ABOUT GAZONGA . . . ER, BUSTI, NEW YORK?

Busti has about 8,000 people and covers 50 square miles.

BUTTERNUTS,
NEW YORK

Not far from the National Baseball Hall of Fame and Museum, nestled near James Fenimore Cooper country, is a town that sounds like: A) A porn film, B) A porn star, C) A very intimate nickname, or D) A failed name for a candy bar?

Butternuts, New York, is named for a creek that runs through town, but the creek, most likely, was named for the local presence of butternut trees and, in particular, an odd formation of three butternut trees growing from one stump, discovered in the area.

These days, the community boasts around 2,000 proud Butternutters, most of whom are white and fairly affluent, according to 2000 census data.

Perhaps, among these Butternutters, is the next Ron Jeremy or Jenna Jameson, working hard to put Butternuts on the map. ⌐

PLEASE PASS THE BUTTERNUTS.

Butternuts, New York, is in New York's Otsego County, in the part of New York that looks and feels nothing like Manhattan.

I CAN'T BELIEVE IT'S NOT BUTTERNUTS.

Butternuts was named for a local stream, but the stream probably got its name from the presence of area butternut trees.

DO BUTTER-NUTTERS EAT NUT-TER BUTTERS?

Probably. They also may have eaten Butternut bars, a chocolate concoction once made by the Hollywood Candy Company.

BUTTZVILLE,
NEW JERSEY

Buttzville may be a delightful community, one of those that gives the Garden State its nickname. It may be filled with smiling folks, nuclear families, old-fashioned values. Heck, someone as wise as Sheriff Andy Taylor may keep the peace in this little corner of New Jersey that's just a whisper away from the Pennsylvania border.

But, but—and it's a *big* but—the town has a name that can't help but make it the butt of numerous jokes told by numerous wags, from Borscht Belt comedians to local high school students. Yo, dude, you're so ugly, you must come from BUTTZVILLE.

The community was not named for anyone's ass. Rather, it was named for Robert Buttz, a man who built a store and hotel in the region. Buttz must have been a putz, though. Picture a guy made fun of all his life who manages to become a bit successful. He decides to corral everyone in his new town under the name Buttzville so that they, too, can be made fun of for life. Butthole.

Nowadays, Buttzville is home to Johnny's, whose sign features a giant wiener and entices hungry customers with the promise of fresh buttermilk. Hmm. Buttermilk in Buttzville underneath a giant wiener. Good times.

Incidentally, Buttzville is just up the road from Hope, New Jersey, as in, "I hope to God I can pick myself out of Buttzville soon." ➔

CAN YOU FIND YOUR BUTTZVILLE WITH BOTH HANDS AND A FLASHLIGHT?

Buttzville is in Warren County, New Jersey, just south of the Pennsylvania border.

WHY DID THEY PICK *BUTTZVILLE*?

The town is named for an early settler, Robert Buttz, who built a store in the area.

WHAT DO YOU NEED TO KNOW ABOUT BUTTZVILLE?

It's home to Johnny's, a fast food establishment featuring weenies and buttermilk. Nutritious and delicious.

CATBRAIN,
ENGLAND

Some towns' names are funny because they sound dirty. Some are funny because they are bizarre. And some make you want to vomit profusely. Surely, Catbrain, a lovely village north of Bristol, is one of the latter.

Questions abound. Are these cat brains just, like, exposed? Are they fried up and served with a nice Chianti? Or are they still inside some feline's head? Who cares? Cat brains are disgusting, wherever they reside. So what possessed some wily Brit to name his town after something revolting? Was it because Shitterton (see page 161) was already taken?

In fact, *Catbrain* is a modernization of the Middle English words *cattes brazen*, which refer to soil found in the region. Catbrain soil tends to be clay-rich and filled with stones.

Catbrain today is associated with car dealerships and a great big shopping mall because it is located along the bustling Cribbs Causeway. If any two enterprises are more targeted toward tiny, cat-brained people, then they are difficult to imagine. ➚

HEY, DOG-FACE, WHERE IS CATBRAIN?

Catbrain is north of Bristol, on the busy Cribbs Causeway.

WHY IS THIS TOWN NAMED FOR CAT BRAINS?

In fact, *Catbrain* is a modernized version of Middle English words that describe the area's rocky, clay-rich soil.

WHAT DO YOU NEED TO KNOW ABOUT CATBRAIN?

The town is the butt of many jokes about small-minded people.

CHRISTMAS,
MICHIGAN

For some, Christmas is a magical time of year, replete with eyes-all-aglow tots and the joy of giving . . . oh, and Jesus fits in there someplace. For others, Christmas is one giant, depressing clusterfuck that can't end soon enough.

If you fall into the latter category—like most normal people—then stay away from the upper peninsula of Michigan. There, you will find a town that celebrates Christmas 365 days a year (except during Leap Year, when it celebrates Christmas 366 days a year).

Christmas, Michigan, has about 400 people who are just nucking futty about this most retail friendly of holidays. And no wonder! The town began when a man from a nearby community built a factory there to produce holiday gifts. The factory is gone, but Christmas lives on . . . ad nauseum.

People send their Christmas cards to Christmas so that they will be postmarked with the town's name. They buy pasty sauce at local merchants. From what we can gather, this is stuff you put on pasties, those tiny bits of material that cover strippers' nipples. And, of course, Santa and Mrs. Claus are always about exhorting people to part with their hard-earned money.

If folks don't want to spend their money on Christmas crap, they can always lose it at the Kewadin Casino, which also calls Christmas home. ↗

HO, HO, HO, WHERE IS CHRISTMAS?

Christmas is on Michigan's Upper Peninsula.

HO, HO, HO, *WHY* CHRISTMAS?

Long, long ago, elves with STDs were quarantined in the area. That's one theory. The other is that long, long ago a man created a tourist trap in the area that specialized in Christmas gifts. That particular tourist trap is gone, replaced by scores of others.

WHAT DO YOU NEED TO KNOW ABOUT CHRISTMAS, HO?

Pasties aren't just nipple-coverings. They're also a kind of British pastry.

CLIMAX AND HIGH POINT,
NORTH CAROLINA

North Carolina is blessed to contain both mountains and the seaside. It has numerous photo-friendly spots, from antebellum mansions to tall skyscrapers to pictures of your kids gamboling along the Carolina Beach shore.

Yet, one of the most photographed sites in the state is along U.S. Highway 220 near Greensboro. It's not that the area contains breathtaking scenery. Nope, it contains an exit sign telling you you're midway between Climax and High Point.

In addition to being a euphemism for *bust a nut*, *climax* also means *high place*. This is what the good folks of the Atlantic & Yadkin Railway had in mind when they named this small community Climax. It was on comparatively high ground, at almost 900 feet above sea level.

The iron horse also was responsible for the naming of nearby High Point. It was at the highest point along the North Carolina Railroad, between Goldsboro and Charlotte. So, in addition to having the world's largest chest of drawers, High Point also has a name that puts some people in mind of Barry White and K-Y Jelly, especially when it is paired with its nearby neighbor, Climax.

So, if you want to be one of the guys who honestly can claim he has brought his woman to Climax, then you should definitely pay this part of North Carolina a visit. Otherwise, you'll be a liar, man. ↗

WHERE CAN I FIND MY CLIMAX?

It's a small community near High Point and Greensboro.

WHY ARE THESE PLACES NAMED AFTER ORGASMS?

They're not. Their names are related to their elevation along railway lines.

WHAT DO I NEED TO KNOW ABOUT CLIMAX?

Most women's are faked.

CLOWNE,
ENGLAND

How does anyone from this small Derbyshire town get a job? "We'd love to hire you, old chap, but you're . . . you're . . . you're a Clowne! Now, piss off."

Named for a Celtic river, *Clun,* Clowne coal helped to fuel the Industrial Revolution, and to this day, it is used to propel all those little Clowne cars into which dozens of Clownes stuff themselves for their morning commutes to whichever employers are willing to endure their zany shenanigans.

Clowne is near many important English sites, such as Sherwood Forest, so it attracts tourists who, presumably, appreciate wake-up calls consisting of a little song, a little dance, a little seltzer down their pants.

It's a charming place. There is absolutely no truth to the rumor that Bozo once vacationed in the town, later telling tripadvisor.com, "Don't bother. This place is a fucking joke." ↗

WHERE DOES ONE CLOWNE AROUND?

Clowne is in Derbyshire County, roughly in the middle of England, far from clown princes of comedy like Prince Charles's kid, you know, the one who likes to dress up like a Nazi?

WHY ARE YOU SUCH A CLOWNE?

The Celtic river, *Clun,* has been changed—in zany, madcap fashion—to *Clowne,* which sometimes is written *Clown* without the "e." What's the matter with you Clownes? Can't you figure out the name of your own towne?

WHAT'S WITH THIS CLOWNE?

Clowne was a small farming community until the Industrial Revolution. Now it's a small, suburban community with a funny name.

COCKBURN,
AUSTRALIA

Do they have weenie roasts in Cockburn, or is the symbolism just too great? You know, "Careful, don't burn my wiener in Cockburn. Oh, wait a minute . . . ." Then the guy's eyes roll up in vicarious pain, and he starts shaking, and another weenie roast has ended in a deluge of psychic sludge. Shudder.

Cockburn, in fact, was named for a British naval hero, Admiral Sir George Cockburn. Cockburn, born 1772, was perhaps most famous for escorting Napoleon into exile after the Battle of Waterloo. Or perhaps he was most famous for having a name that sounded like a singed penis.

Cockburn is a suburb, or one might even consider it an exurb, of Perth, Australia's capital city. Since the town became incorporated in 1971, it has been a bastion of government corruption. The entire town council was let go in 1999, and new corruption charges emerged just eight years later.

It just goes to show you what happens when money burns a hole in a corrupt councilman's cock . . . er, pocket. Shudder. ⬈

WHERE IS COCKBURN?

In your pants, just behind that scorching latte you picked up from Starbucks.

WHY IS IT NAMED FOR BURNING PENISES?

Cockburn is named for Admiral Sir George Cockburn, who escorted Napoleon into exile after Waterloo.

WHAT DO YOU NEED TO KNOW ABOUT COCKBURN?

You should avoid it at all costs because it hurts like a bitch.

COCKERMOUTH,
ENGLAND

Hey, here's an interesting bit of historical trivia! Did you know that the poet William Wordsworth was born in a town that sounds like it's commanding a blow job? It's true! Wordsworth is probably the most famous person born in the tiny, medieval village of Cockermouth.

Actually, to most people today, Wordsworth is the second most famous person to come from this orally-fixated-sounding town. The first is, appropriately enough, Simon Cowell, that a-hole who insults people on *American Idol.* Gosh . . . remember when that show was relevant?

It was almost as long ago as the town of Cockermouth was formed. The Romans once marched through the area and built forts in the region. But the town is most associated with medieval times and maintains a medieval streetscape.

Why did this picturesque village become named for blowjobs? Well, it seems that the town is near the mouth of the Cocker River. Unfortunately, no one who chose the name "Cockermouth" considered that, one day, hundreds of years in the future, some asshole would write a book pointing out that the town's name conjures up images of mouth-on-genital fun.

Oh well. Just remember what Wordsworth said: "Cockermouth, though it sounds like head, / Is a lovely place to make one's bed." And if he *didn't* write that, then he damn sure should have. ↗

> **WHERE IS COCKERMOUTH?**
>
> Cockermouth is at the mouth of England's Cocker River, of course.

> **WHY IS IT NAMED FOR BJS?**
>
> Didn't we just tell you that the town is at the mouth of the Cocker River?

> **WHAT DO YOU NEED TO KNOW ABOUT COCKERMOUTH?**
>
> "Mean" judge Simon Cowell was born there, and so was William Wordsworth.

COCKROACH BAY,
FLORIDA

In the earliest days of the Sunshine State, folks gave pleasant-sounding names to pieces of land that spawned malaria and had more quicksand than stunning ocean views. One place, near Tampa, is exactly the opposite. Cockroach Bay likely got its name from Spanish explorers who thought that the beautiful bay and its surrounding keys were covered with monstrous cockroaches. In fact, these geniuses had discovered horseshoe crabs, which do bare a slight resemblance to a cockroach . . . if you're hammered on Madeira (Mr. PC . . . I *know* that Madeira is made in Portugal, not Spain. Now move on.) Nowadays, the Cockroach Bay area has been turned into a nature preserve, and efforts are being made to undo what development did occur there over the centuries. Cockroach Bay does contain some big cockroaches, but it also has submerged reefs and canoe trails, and it's a fisherman's paradise.

Unlike most aquatic preserves, Cockroach Bay's underwater holdings aren't owned by the state, so it's unlikely that some hotshot politician will allow drilling for baby seals there or whatever other ecological snafus might emerge from a politician's pen. Instead, it's owned by the Tampa Bay Port Authority.

Who knows, though? If baby seals or fossil fuels or polyurethane becomes necessary for making people go fast on highways, the authority may let Cockroach Bay get plowed under. Enjoy those giant (horseshoe) crabs while you can! ↗

I'LL CRUSH YOU LIKE A COCK-A-ROACH.

Cockroach Bay comprises thousands of acres of protected wetlands and undersea outcroppings near Tampa.

HOLY SHIT, THOSE ARE BIG COCKROACHES.

Early Spanish explorers mistook horseshoe crabs for humongous cockroaches. Dumbasses.

WHERE'S MY FLYSWATTER?

Cockroach Bay is home to many species of fish, and it has submerged reefs, perfect for exploring scuba divers.

41

COME BY CHANCE,
AUSTRALIA

Most of the time, you mean to do it. You know, thirty seconds or so after you start, it's all over. You're left with nothing but forced cuddling and a wet spot that both of you try desperately to avoid. If you get right down to it, about the only time you ever really come by chance is if you're having a wet dream . . . or if you're in Australia.

Come by Chance is a town in New South Wales, the country/continent's largest state. At one time, the area contained a well-hidden house of prostitution. Anyone who stumbled upon it could be said to "come by chance."

Okay, that's completely made up. It's more interesting than the actual name origin, though. In truth, George and William Colless were on their way to a spot of land they wished to purchase when they found another large, vacant piece of land. Since the discovery was accidental, the two decided to name their fledgling community Come By Chance.

Only two hundred or so people routinely Come by Chance due to living in the town. All others do so in the middle of the night after watching too much porn. ↗

> **OHHH, I'M COMING!**
>
> Come by Chance is in a heavily forested portion of Australia's New South Wales.

> **COME ON!**
>
> Come by Chance was named for how the town was founded. Its discoverers were on their way to someplace else when they found the land.

> **COME TOGETHER, OVER ME.**
>
> There is actually *another* Come by Chance . . . in Newfoundland.

CONCEPTION,
MISSOURI

Couples spend millions, hell, billions each year to become fertile. I wonder if they're aware of the small town near Kansas City where they're *certain* to find Conception. They can just plop down and, to paraphrase the Beatles, "do it in the road." Nine months later . . . *voila* . . . welcome to the world, little tax write-off!

Conception is named for the local Conception Abbey, a place, apparently, at which monks are impregnated, in extremely miraculous fashion. Why the hell else would the abbey be called *conception*? Huh? Oh, yeah, Mary and Jesus and all that.

Well, anyway, the abbey has been in its current location since 1873. A town grew up around it but never became an official, incorporated town. That honor went to nearby Conception Junction, yet another spot for aspiring parents to have a go at conceiving a small, mewing, puking miracle. Or, just forget about the whole thjng and stick to sex without any consequences. You know…a typical Friday night. ↗

> **WHERE IS CONCEPTION?**
>
> It takes place inside a woman's uterus, right?

> **WHY IS IT NAMED *CONCEPTION*?**
>
> The town is named for Conception Abbey.

> **WHAT DO YOU NEED TO KNOW ABOUT CONCEPTION?**
>
> It can be easily prevented by practicing safe sex.

CONVICT LAKE,
CALIFORNIA

California is known for its scenic beauty and for its crime. Therefore, is it any wonder that both would be combined somewhere in the state? Of course not! Smack dab in the middle of Mono County (see page 136) is Convict Lake.

The lake itself isn't really anything special. What makes it truly breathtaking is the presence behind it of snow-capped mountains, including Mount Morrison, named for a guy involved in the incident that gave the lake its name.

It seems that crime in California did not originate in the twentieth century with Charles Manson, the Zodiac Killer, Richard Ramirez, the mob, and various fat cats who bilk little old ladies out of their life savings.

In the nineteenth century, a group of convicts escaped from jail in Carson City, Nevada. They made their way west, until they met a posse led by Sheriff Robert Morrison, at the site of Convict Lake. During the melee that followed, Morrison was killed.

Since that time, Convict Lake has endured further abuse by being used as a backdrop in such awful movies as *Star Trek: Insurrection*. And, come to think of it, shouldn't the locals consider changing the name?

Convict Lake conjures up, well, convicts and prison life and dropping the soap and nonconsensual anal sex. Perhaps they should consider something else, like, say, Giant Titz Lake or Lake Humpalot? Just some suggestions. ↗

WHERE DOES CONVICT LAKE HIDE OUT?

Convict Lake is in Mono County, California, just across the border from Nevada.

WHY IS IT CALLED CONVICT LAKE?

The name is due to a nineteenth-century incident involving convicts and a sheriff's posse.

WHAT DO YOU NEED TO KNOW ABOUT CONVICT LAKE?

This scenic spot has been featured in a few films. Some, like *How the West Was Won*, really aren't that bad.

COWLIC,
ARIZONA

Dang, dude, your hair is sticking up everywhere! Well, that got *most* of it, but you've still got one big ol' Alfalfa Switzer lick coming right up from your forehead like some sort of ugly-ass unicorn's horn. Nope, still there. Well, don't worry about it. No one will even notice.

In fact, you might want to go to a place in Arizona that is one giant Cowlic, sticking up out of the desert, not far from Tucson. And you're in luck! You can't spell for shit and neither can they! They left that final "k" off the end of their town's name.

In Cowlic, all the haircuts are bad, the barbers pure evil, and the mousse nonexistent. Perhaps it's the desert wind, blowing constantly, that causes 365 bad hair days in Cowlic. Maybe everyone's just butt ugly? Who knows?

Well, it might make all these folks feel somewhat better if they know that their town is not, in fact, named for cowlicks. In fact, *cowlic* is a Tohono O'odham—or local Native American tribe—word that means "hill" or "little mountain." Since the town of Cowlic sits at an elevation of over 2,000 feet, the name makes perfect sense.

Of course, it might also make sense because, as noted, everyone there is butt ugly. So, go visit. You should fit in quite nicely. ↗

> **WHERE IS COWLIC?**
>
> Until you started losing your hair, you probably found them all over your head.

> **WHY IS IT NAMED FOR A BAD HAIR DAY?**
>
> *Cowlic* is a word that means "little mountain" or "hill" in the language of a local Native American tribe.

> **WHAT DO YOU NEED TO KNOW ABOUT COWLIC?**
>
> Surely not *all* of the people there are butt ugly.

COXSACKIE,
NEW YORK

Folks in this Hudson River town have Native Americans and Dutch settlers to thank for a name that sounds like "ball sack." And, if it makes the folks in town feel any better, then they can focus on the fact that the town also is known for the Coxsackievirus (no joke), which is passed orally (!) or through fecal matter (!) and can lead to meningitis. The virus was first detected in Coxsackie in the 1940s.

Long before Coxsackie was home to viruses passed via people who don't understand the antiseptic qualities of hand-washing, it was settled by the Dutch as part of the country's New Netherlands development. One of its earliest settlers was Pieter Bronck, for whom New York City's Bronx borough was named.

Coxsackie is both a town and a village, both of which share this name. Why did the fine folks of these two rural communities decide they were happy to be named for ball sacks? Well . . . there's no good answer for that. As for what the name *Coxsackie* means, there's not a consensus on *that* either. Most agree that it is some sort of amalgamation of Dutch and Native American languages, though who provided the "cox" and who provided the "sackie" is unclear.

No one, Dutch or Native American, is particularly eager to claim either. The resulting word, *Coxsackie*, is typically said to translate to "hoot of the owl" or something similar. Maybe the locals will wise up, stop being known as *ball sacks*, and change their name to *Hooterville*. ↗

WHERE IS COXSACKIE?

Dangling under your Johnson, if you've got a pair.

WHY IS IT NAMED FOR BALL SACKS?

Apparently, *Coxsackie* is a Native American/Dutch mishmash of a word that means "owl's hoot."

WHAT DO YOU NEED TO KNOW ABOUT COXSACKIE?

In addition to putting one in mind of a ball sack, the town gave rise to the Coxsackievirus.

CRACKPOT,
ENGLAND

The British Isles have a Twatt, a Muff, a Catbrain, a Shitterton, and even a Clowne (see pages 181, 145, 35, and 161, respectively). Is it any wonder that you can also find a Crackpot in the motherland? Besides, if you live in the middle of a nowhere like Crackpot, then you can't help but turn to crack, pot, meth, booze, or whatever else will keep you from getting so bored that you just swallow Drano and die.

Crackpot, in England's North Yorkshire County, derives from an Old English word and a contemporaneous Viking word. The Old English word is *kraka,* which means "crow." Apparently, crows are common in the area. The Viking word is *pot,* which refers to deep holes in the limestone of the area. It may also refer to the aforementioned marijuana and crack since that's about all there is for teens to do in this crappy burg: smoke a lot of dope, hit the crack pipe, and go spelunking. What is *spelunking*? Cave diving. If you were in Muff, Ireland (see page 145), you could go Muff diving. But since you're in Crackpot, you have to settle for cave diving in Crackpot Cave.

Inside, past "Knee-Wrecker Passage" (no lie), you'll find an excellent example of a limestone column, made over gazillions of years when a stalactite (the things that hang down) met a stalagmite (the things that grow up from the ground). Since viewing a limestone column is what passes for fun in Crackpot, why the fuck *wouldn't* young people opt for pipes and blunts? ↗

WHERE'S MY CRACK(POT), HO?

Crackpot is in North Yorkshire, England, near Crackpot Cave, of course.

WHY IS IT NAMED FOR DRUGS, OR POSSIBLY, BENNY HILL?

Kraka is an Old English word meaning "crow." *Pot* is a Viking word meaning "serious buzz," or, perhaps, "deep crevices in rock." Take your choice.

WHAT DO YOU NEED TO KNOW ABOUT CRACKPOT?

It is not named for crack or pot. It contains a cave. It is a boring place.

CRAPO,
MARYLAND

People who live in the United States' various Pleasantvilles, Pleasant Gardens, and Greenvilles probably think their hometowns are crappy places to live. They bitch about how there's nothing to do there and about their stupid neighbors and those damn kids and on and on and on. They've got it all wrong. They could be living in a *truly* crappy place.

Near the beautiful Eastern Shore of the state, Crapo, Maryland actually honors frogs, both the kinds that hop and the kinds that live in a snooty, Jerry Lewis-loving country. You see, *crapaud* is French for "toad" (I know toads and frogs aren't the same thing. Just go with it, smartass.).

Voila! *Crapo* is pronounced *CRAY-poh* by the locals. Fantastic! One more thing to hate about the French. ↗

WHERE IS THIS CRAPO PLACE?

Crapo is near Maryland's Eastern Shore.

WHY IS IT SO CRAPO?

Crapaud is French for "shitty, existentialist, ennui-inducing films." Oh, wait. No, in fact, it's French for "toad." Apparently, the area is filled with frogs . . . the kind that hop, not the ones in berets.

WHAT CRAPO STUFF DO YOU NEED TO KNOW?

Don't have a local open a can of whoop-ass on you. The town is pronounced *CRAY-poh*.

CROOK,
COLORADO

At first, it would seem that this small Colorado town is named for a thief. Perhaps, one might think, there was a major railroad jacking in the area, or maybe some storied thief or gang—the Daltons, the Jameses—came through as they pillaged and plundered.

But, no. This town was not named for *that* kind of crook. Nor, it turns out, was it named for its populace. Nope, folks in this town are as honest—and dishonest—as people anywhere else. Sure, they steal office supplies from their workplace or take an extra newspaper out of the machine from time to time, but overall, they're law-abiding citizens.

Crook was, in fact, named for General George Crook, a veteran of the Civil War. So, the town is named for a hero, right? Wrong, smartass! Guess what?! Crook *was* a crook.

After he spent his time fighting Johnny Reb, he spent the rest of his career going after "bad injuns." He "distinguished" himself by leading troops that killed thirty-six Lakota at the Battle of Rosebud and as many as a thousand Sioux during the Great Sioux War (that's the one that included the Battle of Little Big Horn, dumbass).

The bottom line? Folks who had lived on land for thousands of years had it stolen from them by a Crook! Talk about irony! Oh well. Nowadays, Crook, Colorado, is a town of about 128. Not surprisingly, it's 100 percent white! Way to go, General Crook! ↗

I AM NOT A CROOK!
Crook is in Colorado's Logan County.

DID RICHARD NIXON LIVE THERE?
No, it's named for General George Crook, veteran of the Civil War and the so-called Indian Wars.

WHAT DO YOU NEED TO KNOW ABOUT CROOK?
It's lily white.

CUMMING,
GEORGIA

There are some folks living near Atlanta who make Sting, and other practitioners of Tantric sex, look like total amateurs. That's right. Sting may last for hours, but these folks *never* stop Cumming. They just keep on Cumming and Cumming and Cumming. It's pretty gross, actually.

Cumming was not, in fact, named for the way adolescents spell the result of lovemaking. It was, instead, named in honor of William Cumming, Augusta native and hero of the War of 1812.

Long before it earned its ejaculation-de-plume, Cumming was home to the Cherokee, who co-existed with European settlers . . . until gold was discovered in Georgia. Then it was "Bye bye, Red Man." The Cherokee may not have been Cumming, but they sure were fucked.

Nowadays, Cumming is, appropriately, a bedroom community for nearby Atlanta, with some 5,000 residents, all of whom, we're sure, just love Cumming. ⌐

I'M CUMMING.
Cumming is in Forsyth County, near Atlanta.

HE'S CUMMING.
The town was named in honor of a War of 1812 hero, William Cumming.

SHE'S CUMMING.
Oprah once featured the town on her show because it has an uneasy history of black-white relations. No word on whether or not she had a Big O there.

CUNTER,
SWITZERLAND

If you needed any proof that Europeans are more cosmopolitan than Americans you need only look toward Switzerland, home of secret bank accounts, peace, skiing, and a city named Cunter.

All right, all right, this delightful part of Switzerland isn't named for vaginas nor is it named for Hillary Clinton (if you're conservative) or Ann Coulter (if you're liberal). It's just a Romansh word for "in the direction of."

Romansh, since you probably don't know, is one of Switzerland's four official languages. There, dumbass! You learned something . . . from a dirty book! Cunter is midway between two larger places: Tiefencastel and Savognin. Hence, "in the direction of."

You'll find about three hundred Cunterites in Cunter. Oddly enough, however, there are more men than women in Cunter. Who knew? ↗

HE'S A CUNTER.

Cunter, Switzerland is in the *canton* (state) of Graubunden, near the Italian border.

SHE'S A CUNTER.

Cunter is Romansh for "in the direction of." Romansh is one of Switzerland's four official languages, which you already knew . . . right?

WOULDN'T YOU LIKE TO BE A CUNTER, TOO?

Cunter has grown during the last decade, due to people moving there from other countries.

CUT AND SHOOT,
TEXAS

Pastors who can't keep their hands, and other body parts, off the ladies are nothing new. Long before Jimmy Swaggart—remember *that* sleazeball?—told his followers, crocodile tears flowing forth, "I have sinned against you," preachers have been, um, dipping their chalices.

For whatever reason, some women find a "man of God" indescribably sexy, and they will forsake a slew of commandments in order to know him . . . in the Biblical sense. A randy pastor and some horny local wives are behind the legend of the odd Texas town name *Cut and Shoot*.

As legend has it, a local pastor was becoming better known for his bedside manner than for his preaching. Tongues, and other body parts, wagged. Menfolk began to get pretty pissed off.

One Sunday, somebody said something, leading someone else to say something and yadda yadda yadda. As a group, the men left the church in order to find weapons in order to "cut and shoot" the pastor. History doesn't record what happened next, but it's unlikely that particular pastor spent any more time talking about such religious subjects as missionary positions.

Other local legends say the dispute was over a church expansion or land claims among some members, but stories of the Lord-lovin' Lothario remain most popular. ↗

> **CUT IT OUT.**
> Cut and Shoot is about fifty miles from Houston.

> **AW, SHOOT.**
> Several legends abound related to the town's odd name, but the most popular involves a randy pastor, horny wives, and pissed off husbands.

> **CUT THE SHIT . . . ER, SHOOT.**
> The community did not become an incorporated city until 2006.

DEAD HORSE POINT STATE PARK,
UTAH

We're all for history. History is a good thing, especially colorful yarns that instill wonder in young tykes' eyes as they sit around the campfire. But you still have to wonder about the douchebag who opted to name a beautiful state park after a bunch of dead animals. And not just any animals. After all, one might be tempted to visit "Dead Skunk Park" because the name suggests that you won't have to worry about seeing any of these stinky creatures. Or you'd be intrigued by "Dead Walrus Park" because you'd be shocked at the thought that walruses might once have migrated through what is now the Utah desert. But no. This park near Moab, Utah is named after an animal that most people, especially most children, like: Dead Horse Point.

Why? Well, it seems that, long ago, wild mustangs held sway over the present spot of the state park. As people moved to the area, they found that the twisty ranges of the park and its canyons created a natural corral into which the mustangs could be led in order to be tamed. One group of maverick mustangs was left behind in the corral, and, being rather stupid, the horses stayed put, even after the corral's fence was left open. The horses died of thirst while in sight of the Colorado River. Stupid horses! No wonder their proof of Darwin's theories has caused the park to be named in their "honor." ⟩

WHERE IS THIS DISGUSTINGLY NAMED PLACE?

Dead Horse Point State Park is near Moab, Utah.

WHY DOES IT HAVE THIS RETCH-INDUCING SOBRIQUET?

The name is related to a legend involving the wild mustangs once found in the area.

WHAT DO YOU NEED TO KNOW ABOUT DEAD HORSE POINT STATE PARK?

Don't eat the s'mores! You don't know what's in 'em!

DEAD WOMEN CROSSING,
OKLAHOMA

Psycho killers have fascinated us—as long as we're not the victims, naturally—for generations. And, surely, a place with a name this grim must have been the site of some particularly brutal murders, right? Wrong. The body count is just two: one murder and one suicide.

Around the turn of the last century, a woman named Katy James disappeared, her body later found by fishermen. Whodunit? No one ever knew for sure. Another woman, prostitute Fanny Norton, wound up with James's child. Most likely, Norton and James's estranged husband were in cahoots and yada yada yada.

Whether from guilt, shame, or indigestion, Norton wound up killing herself. She later was found guilty of the murder of James. Possible motive? Money. A love triangle. Who knows? Then, as now, girl fights can get brutal.

Supposedly, if you stand at the bridge in Dead Women Crossing, you can hear a woman calling desperately for her baby. Some say you hear old-fashioned wagon wheels rolling by. Of course, most who say these things are teenagers on weekend benders replete with Everclear-spiked oranges and loads of shitty weed.

Whatever you do, if you are from this small Oklahoma community, don't go to college and admit this to a girl you meet at a party. You will *not* get laid, and she is likely to run screaming. ↗

WHERE IS DEAD WOMEN CROSSING?

Dead Women Crossing is a small community some thirty miles from Oklahoma City.

WHY IS IT CALLED DEAD WOMEN CROSSING?

A local crime, which resulted in two dead women, gave rise to the name.

WHAT DO YOU NEED TO KNOW ABOUT DEAD WOMEN CROSSING?

Supposedly, the place is haunted. It's a place drunken teenage guys take girls in hopes of scaring them enough to get, at least, to third base.

DEVIL'S DYKE,
ENGLAND

Perhaps the butchest spot on the planet can be found in Sussex, England. You would have to be bullest of butch to be the Devil's Dyke.

Actually, once upon a time, a *dyke* was something you put your finger in. Nowadays, you can *still* put your finger in one, but, well . . . You get the picture. The Devil's Dyke is a v-shaped valley in southern England. Legend has it that the valley was formed by the devil. The devil, who is said to hate all things holy and good, was upset that Sussex had so many churches, preaching the gospels of class stratification and obeisance to authority and whatever else the churches in England profess.

The devil decided to build a trench to allow the sea to flow into Sussex and destroy all the churches. The devil could not, however, complete his task. His digging awoke an old woman (the Devil's Dyke, perhaps?!?), who lit a candle, which caused a rooster to crow. As a result, the devil thought morning had come, and, in this particular myth, the devil cannot perform his evil deeds during daylight hours. The trench was left incomplete, saving the Sussex churches.

Another story suggests that the devil formed the valley after turning himself into a giant goat. He intended to stomp all the churches into oblivion. As he got closer to the sea, he became concerned that his coat would get wet. Remember . . . vanity is one of the seven deadly sins. He fled the area, leaving only a giant, v-shaped print. ↗

WHERE IS DEVIL'S DYKE?

This oddly named valley can be found in Sussex, near the southern coast of England.

WHY IS IT NAMED FOR THE DEROGATORY TERM FOR AN EXTREMELY BUTCH LESBIAN?

In fact, Devil's Dyke was, according to myth, formed by the devil and not by any lesbians.

WHAT DO YOU NEED TO KNOW ABOUT DEVIL'S DYKE?

It was formed during the Ice Age.

DEVIL'S TRAMPING GROUND,
SILER CITY, NORTH CAROLINA

The devil, as everyone knows, spends most of his time plotting how to gain more souls. That's his job. And he's damn good at it! But even a hard-working soul-stealer has to have some "me" time. Where does Satan spend it? Apparently, he favors a little spot near Siler City, North Carolina.

The Devil's Tramping Ground is a perfect circle with a diameter of around forty feet. No plants will grow within it, and, supposedly, even the most docile pets will claw at you if you try to take them into the circle. One-toothed locals will tell you that nothing will remain on the Devil's Tramping Ground. In other words, if you place, say, a bunch of beer bottles inside the circle one night, they will be gone by morning.

Maybe it's just due to alcoholic blackouts? Or maybe the devil, as bad as he is, still believes that cleanliness is next to godliness. Hey, wasn't he once God's brightest angel or something?

Some whackos—a technical term for paranormal investigators—claim the Devil's Tramping Ground is a crop circle because, after all, where else in the universe would E.T.'s want to go to party but the middle of fucking nowhere in Redneckville, U.S.A.? ↗

WHERE THE DEVIL IS IT?

The Devil's Tramping Ground is near Siler City, North Carolina, AKA, "The Armpit of America."

HOW THE DEVIL DID IT GET ITS NAME?

The Devil's Tramping Ground is, supposedly, created by the constant "tramping" of Satan. Satan visits when he's not telling Sarah Palin which career move to take next.

WHAT THE DEVIL DO YOU NEED TO KNOW ABOUT IT?

The Devil's Tramping Ground is a perfect circle, about 40 feet in diameter, on which nothing grows. Some believe it was formed by Lucifer himself, who uses the spot for pacing around as he thinks of new ways to gain human souls. Others believe it's a crop circle.

DICK PEAKS,
ANTARCTICA

Antarctica . . . the final frontier. A place of extreme cold, horny penguins, and two giant penises sticking up from the ice like X-rated monoliths.

Okay, Dick Peaks don't really look like dicks. They're just two generic Antarctic mountains, standing near the larger Mount Humble. How did they receive their phallic names, you ask?

Was it someone fed up with cold, cursing the dicks who had sent him to Antarctica in the first place, to do surveying or whatever the hell else it is one does in a continent that's mostly ice and which boasts temperatures far, far below zero?

No. The mountains were named in 1960 for a weather observer whose last name was Dick. Dick, who spent his time recording the continent's wind speeds and killing temperatures from Antarctica's Mawson station, must have become positively engorged by the honor. ⊅

▶ WHAT A DICK.
Dick Peaks is in Antarctica, in the middle of nowhere, like every other place in Antarctica.

▶ YOU'RE A DICK.
Dick Peaks were named for Mr. Dick, a weather observer at Antarctica's Mawson station.

▶ DON'T BE A DICK.
Unless you are obsessed with penguins (and you know who you are, weirdo), then stay the fuck out of Antarctica.

DICKSHOOTER,
IDAHO

God, where does one start? With a reference to former Vice President Dick Cheney and his "hunting accident" that resulted in the non-fatal shooting of a Cheney friend. Nope, that happened in Texas. How about with the way all men in the following town wince when asked where they're from? Yeah, that works. Welcome to Dickshooter, Idaho!

No, a cringe-inducing incident involving guns and penises did not leave its permanent mark on this community in the extreme southwestern corner of Idaho, nor is this a favorite filming spot for the porn industry. The rugged, middle-of-pretty-much-nowhere community was founded by a guy named Dick Shooter. The man is gone, but his Dickshooter lives on.

Nowadays, Dickshooter is a sparsely populated community popular for outdoor sports like fishing, camping, and hunting. Hey, watch where yer pointing that rifle! ↗

WHERE IS DICKSHOOTER?

Dickshooter is in Owyhee County, Idaho, which is adjacent to Oregon and Nevada.

HOW DID DICK-SHOOTER GET ITS NAME?

A man named Dick Shooter. Honest.

WHAT DO YOU NEED TO KNOW ABOUT DICKSHOOTER?

Dickshooter is a sparsely populated spot popular for outdoor pursuits.

DIKSHIT,
INDIA

In India, it is an honor to be a Dikshit. Most with this surname belong to the Brahmin class. Hindu society is divided into four castes, with Brahmins occupying the top rung of the social ladder. Think of Brahmins as equivalent to people in America who are descended from families who sailed on the Mayflower. You know, "Boston Brahmins."

So, Dikshits are among the Indian upper crust. It's no surprise that a town was named after this class. After all, *dikshit* derives from a Sanskrit word referring to religious initiations. Dikshit families have ancestors who were, most likely, priests or religious scholars. The village of Dikshit either was founded by Dikshits or once was home to religious festivals.

There's just one problem with being a Diskhit or with living in Dikshit: The English language.

You see, in English the word *dikshit* is inherently funny. It makes one think of the results of anal sex, for example. Or, it just makes one think of two words that adults try not to use around small children: *dick* and *shit*. Or, it makes one think of the word *dipshit*, which refers to someone one considers stupid and incompetent.

English speakers have made a laughingstock of Dikshit and of Dikshits. How sad. Nowadays, most Dikshits are discreetly changing their name to "Dixit," which isn't nearly as funny. Still, you'll know a Dikshit when you see one. ↗

WHERE IS DIKSHIT?
It's in India, you Dikshit.

WHY DOES IT HAVE SUCH A FUNNY NAME?
In India, *Dikshit* is a family name typically indicating someone as a Brahmin, basically the upper class of India.

WHAT DO YOU NEED TO KNOW ABOUT DIKSHIT?
Goddamn, it's a funny name!

DILDO,
NEWFOUNDLAND

A Canadian magazine focused on one Newfoundland community's beauty, naming the spot one of the prettiest in the entire country. And little wonder! The spot has a tranquil bay, delightfully lived-in architecture, and loads of bucolic splendor, all of which would make for a romantic getaway. Surely, any mademoiselle would be delighted to be whisked away to explore Dildo.

No one is quite sure how this small community in Newfoundland earned its name, but theories abound. Theory One: Dildo was named for a Spanish sailor who long ago explored the region. Theory Two: Dildo is named for a long, phallic cylinder that is part of a ship. Theory Three: Dildo is a no-longer-used word for a song's chorus. Shakespeare used *dildo* in this sense at least once. Theory Four: Dildo actually refers to a dick or at least to a dick-like object . . . not to be confused with the appearance of your average Blue Dog Democrat.

You see, *dildo* has meant "penis-like-thing" since the seventeenth century. Dildo is on a peninsula, and, in fact, it does look very much like a dick on a map. Perhaps bawdy sailors, long ago, just decided to call a spade a spade.

Who knows? All that's important is that it's a nice place. Ladies, enjoy getting to know your Dildo! ↗

WHERE IS MY DILDO?

The dog got ahold of it. It's underneath the bureau.

WHY IS DILDO NAMED AFTER A FAKE PENIS?

Many possibilities exist, most of which have to do with the shape of the peninsula on which Dildo sits.

WHAT DO YOU NEED TO KNOW ABOUT DILDO?

It's one of the loveliest spots in Canada. It nearly always produces an orgasm.

DING DONG,
TEXAS

Who cares how gay it sounds? There's no better snacking than cream-filled Ding Dongs. Rich, chocolate goodness that disseminates lighter-than-air white cream. Mmm. They're so good that somebody ought to name a freaking town after them. Oh, wait! Someone did! It's in Texas.

Actually, it's an urban myth that Ding Dong was named for the Hostess treat or for a man's penis. The myth probably comes from folks in the town itself, who have developed a sense of humor about their community's odd, dick- and snack-food-related name.

In fact, Ding Dong traces itself to early settlers Zulis and Bert Bell. The Bells hired a painter to create a sign with two bells on it for the store they planned to open in the burgeoning community. The artist added the onomatopoeic flourish of a "ding dong" emanating from the bells.

The store owners were forgotten, but their ding dongs remained. The town grew up around the shop and, rather than picking the perfectly acceptable name "Bell," residents opted to call themselves Ding Dongs. ↗

WHERE IS MY DING DONG?

It's no surprise YOU'VE got to ask.

IS THIS TOWN NAMED FOR A PENIS? OR FOR A CREAM-FILLED TREAT?

Ding Dong is, in fact, named for a sign that once existed in town. Two early settlers with the last name of Bell opened a store in the area. Their sign featured two bells pealing forth a cheery "ding dong." Townsfolk, perhaps unaware of the double entendre, chose to call their community Ding Dong.

WHAT DO YOU NEED TO KNOW ABOUT DING DONG?

It's one of humankind's greatest snack foods. It's slang for male genitalia. It's a small town in Texas that is *not* named for snack foods or for male genitalia.

DISAPPOINTMENT CREEK,
ALASKA

Some things are just a disappointment: finding out that your garage band will never make it out of the garage, discovering that the woman of your dreams is really the woman of your nightmares, realizing that adulthood is just a series of bland or debilitating disappointments.

Maybe what you need is a quick trip to Alaska. There, amid ice and millions of acres of nothing, you'll find the perfect place to drown yourself . . . er, to drown your sorrows: Disappointment Creek.

The twenty-five-mile-long creek was named by a geologist who spent a long time following the stream, only to find that it did not lead to a pass through the nearby DeLong Mountains.

When the geologist, W. T. Foran, found that he was following a dead end, he probably considered calling the damn thing Motherfucker Creek or Shit Creek (which would make sense; after all he *was* up shit creek). Instead, Foran decided to take the high road and simply note his disappointment . . . for all time. ↗

WHAT A DISAPPOINTMENT.

Disappointment Creek is one hundred miles from the Arctic settlement of Wainwright.

DON'T DISAPPOINT ME.

Disappointment Creek was considered a disappointment by a geologist who surveyed it because the stream did not lead to a mountain pass.

GREAT . . . ANOTHER DISAPPOINTMENT.

The United States has a total of thirteen creeks named *Disappointment*. They should all just kill themselves and get it over with.

DISAPPOINTMENT ISLANDS,
FRENCH POLYNESIA

You know how your folks are always saying you're a disappointment, just because you have no job, no life, and no significant other? Well, you're in luck. You can move out of their basement and head for a spot tailor-made for you: The Disappointment Islands.

The islands sound pretty nice, actually. They're a series of atolls, which means each island encircles a lagoon. But someone, apparently, found them a disappointment. Perhaps it was the fact that they're owned by the French, a notoriously snarky and supercilious bunch. Or perhaps it's the fact that the islands are not hospitable for human occupation.

In fact, the Disappointment Islands gained their name from one of two possible sources. One legend has it that Magellan (the first to circumnavigate the globe) found the islands a disappointment because they did not contain a fresh-water source. Another story holds that British explorer, John Byron, named the islands because the natives were so unfriendly. Hey, maybe they were already French!

Nowadays, the islands are sparsely inhabited. Maybe it's because the largest island, which some do not even believe belongs to the group, is named for vomit: Puka-Puka. ↗

WHERE ARE THE DISAPPOINTMENT ISLANDS?

The islands are a subgroup of the Tuamoto Archipelago, the world's largest archipelago, which is part of French Polynesia. Duh!

WHY ARE THEY SUCH A DISAPPOINTMENT?

Some contend explorer Ferdinand Magellan named them for their lack of water. Others believe inhospitable natives gave rise to the name.

WHAT DO YOU NEED TO KNOW ABOUT THE DISAPPOINTMENT ISLANDS?

They're a big disappointment, so you'll have something in common with them.

DISH,
TEXAS

Do you remember when sports stadiums had real names that honored real people? But why play ball at, say, Ebbets Field or Dodger Stadium when you can play at U.S. Cellular Field (the Chicago White Sox), Citizens Bank Park (the Philadelphia Phillies), or even PETCO Park (the San Diego Padres)? Those names make people think of business, and business makes people want to spend money on ancillary garbage like hats, bobbleheads, pennants, and so on.

But the commercialization of an entire town . . . no self-respecting community would stand for *that* shit, right? Wrong again, motherfucker! Perhaps the first to forego tradition for a publicity stunt was Truth or Consequences, New Mexico (see page 179). But, you know what? They didn't really get a *damn* for changing their name. Suckers!

The fine folks of erstwhile Clark, Texas were much smarter. *Clark* was simply the name of the town's first mayor, and the town wasn't even born until 2000. In 2005, the fine folks of Clark traded a tribute to a town founder for thirty pieces of silver . . . oops, no, wait. They got something much better: Free cable for ten years! The name of the town is DISH in all capital letters. That's because it was named for the DISH Network, a provider of cable satellite television. The folks in DISH now get free basic cable *and* free DVR? Christ, who wouldn't piss all over tributes and tradition for free cable? This is America, goddammit! ↗

WHERE IS DISH?

DISH is in Denton County, Texas, not far from the Oklahoma border.

WHY IS IT NAMED DISH?

So the folks in town could receive *free* basic cable and DVR from the DISH Network.

WHAT DO YOU NEED TO KNOW ABOUT DISH?

Sell out? Who are you calling a sell out? Like you wouldn't do the same damn thing for free basic cable!

DISS,
ENGLAND

People tend to think the "Old Country" is just that: old, out of step with modern times, stuck in some renaissance fair version of the past. Well, you couldn't be more wrong. In fact, how dare you diss England? On second thought, go ahead and diss England because it's going to Diss your ass right back.

Diss, for the uninitiated, is a term borrowed by wiggers from hip-hop. It is short for *disrespect,* and to *diss* someone is to insult him or her, as in, "You sure are a stupid a-hole, bruh." But that's not all Diss is. Nope.

It's also a town of some 7,000 souls in the town of Norfolk. Folks in this progressive town anticipated the term "diss" centuries before it was popularized by white people who pretend to have something in common with the culture of African-American, and presumably, African-British men and women.

The fine folks of Diss walk around, adding "yo, dawg, your mama gives good head" and "hey, bruh, your sister was good last night" to the traditional British greetings of "pip pip" and "cheeri-o." Everyone laughs at the wit because, after all, this is DISS.

Some folks in town would probably argue that *diss* is, in fact, a Norman (?) or Anglo-Saxon (?) or Viking (?) term for "village of the dancing horse." How did a dancing horse get involved with Diss? Who the hell knows? Who the hell cares? What . . . you trying to Diss me, yo? ↗

WHERE IS DISS?

Diss is a town near Norfolk and Suffolk, England.

WHY IS IT NAMED AFTER A HIP-HOP TERM FOR PUTTING SOMEONE DOWN VIA VERBAL BADINAGE?

Diss apparently is a modernization of a word from some older language (opinions differ on which language) that means "village of the dancing horse."

WHAT DO YOU NEED TO KNOW ABOUT DISS?

Nothing. You already get Dissed enough.

DIX,
NEBRASKA

Here's the odd thing about Dix. It's not that the community sounds like it was named after several penises, although that *is* weird. After all, how many guys on a blind date are going to be pleased to announce they're from Dix? Maybe it gets the ladies interested. You know . . . does he have more than one? Could be interesting. OMG! Who knows?

Nope, the odd thing about Dix is that it is *not* named for some guy with that last name who, say, built a general store around which the community grew as many of the towns in this book were so named. And if Dix, Nebraska had earned its sobriquet the same way, well then its name would sound funny but would be perfectly reasonable.

Dix was, instead, named for Dixon, Illinois. The Nebraskan community *chose* a name that sounds like a bunch of penises?!? They could have just called the place Dixon, Nebraska, but *no*. They didn't want their Dix-*on* anything, but they did want to be Dix. Weird.

For that matter, what's so great about Dixon? True, it was the boyhood home of Ronald Reagan, but he would just have been a young man when Dix, Nebraska was formed in the nineteenth century. He wouldn't have been a successful B-list actor, much less a hippie-hating California governor or Communist-hating president, at that time.

No . . . it's just one more puzzling thing about Dix. But pity this poor Nebraskan town. It's a small community, and it looks like Dix is (are?) shrinking. ↗

WHERE IS DIX?

Ha! Ha! Ha! Ahem. Sorry. Nebraska.

WHY IS IT NAMED FOR PENISES?

It's actually named after Dixon, Illinois. For some reason, the folks in Nebraska preferred to drop part of the name and just be Dix.

WHAT DO YOU NEED TO KNOW ABOUT DIX?

The less you know about Dix the better.

DONG,
SOUTH KOREA

South Korea doesn't possess just one Dong. The country is filled with Dongs of varying sizes. Big or small, you won't hear South Koreans complaining about the size of their Dongs because they're a "can do" sort of people. Besides, it's not the size of the boat, it's the motion in the ocean . . . or something to that effect.

South Korea's picturesque Dongs are not located in one place. You will find Dongs by the river, Dongs near urban areas, and Dongs out in the country. In fact, drive a few miles in any direction, and you're certain to come upon a Dong.

So . . . has this joke been worn out enough yet? In South Korea, a *Dong* is the smallest level of urban government to have its own representation in the country. In English, the word often is translated as *neighborhood*.

Each Dong has its own staff (naturally!), working to ensure that each Dong is taken care of by the state. How are the Dong's sewers? How are the Dong's roads? Can you get help with your Dong when you need it?

North Korea has its Dongs as well, but North Korea keeps its Dongs hidden. The country is, of course, notoriously secret, and it wouldn't do to have information about North Korean Dongs in the hands of the West. ➤

DONG, WHERE IS MY AUTOMOBILE?

Dongs are found throughout South Korea.

WHY IS IT CALLED DONG?

A Dong is, basically, a small urban neighborhood.

WHAT DO YOU NEED TO KNOW ABOUT DONG?

We're sure you already know everything you need to know about other people's Dongs.

DUMBELL,
WYOMING

Some might say anyone who lives in Wyoming is a dumbbell. After all, it's the least populous of the lower forty-eight states. It's full of all kinds of nothing. And its largest city is barely large enough to be called a city.

Sure, if you're a fan of wide-open spaces, then Wyoming is for you. As for the rest of us, we'll take states where you can find a good cup of coffee, some nightlife, and more women than cattle.

Is it any wonder, then, that Wyoming is home to a town called *Dumbell*? Is it, for that matter, any surprise that these dumbbells can't even *spell* "dumbbell"? Hello! There are *two* b's in the word! Doesn't this just prove that the town is full of, well, dumbbells?!?

The town was named for the dumbbell brand of a local rancher named Philip Vetter. *He* is, presumably, not to blame for the misspelling. In fact, one wonders how he responded to the "honor" bestowed on him by his fellow townsfolk.

"Well, yeah, I'm pleased you want to name the community after me, but, um, 'Dumbell' may not be the, uh, brightest choice."

No one listened, and now there's a great big Dumbell, smack dab in the middle of a state filled with dumbbells. ↗

HEY, DUMBELL, WHERE YOU AT?

Dumbell is in Park County, Wyoming. Where is Park County? Shit, who knows? Nobody lives in Wyoming anyway.

WHY IS IT NAMED DUMBELL?

A local rancher had a dumbbell-shaped brand, but, for some reason, locals misspelled the word *dumbbell*. Oh, wait. There was a good reason. They're *stupid*.

WHAT DO YOU NEED TO KNOW ABOUT DUMBELL?

Folks there can't spell for shit.

ECLECTIC,
ALABAMA

Wow. Imagine our surprise when we learned that, not only do Alabamians know the word *eclectic* but they also named a community after it. Of course, they may have thought they were naming their town *electric* or *cleric* or something. After all, this *is* Alabama.

Now look . . . we are just having fun at this delightful state's expense. Of course, the state that brought us George Wallace, Bull Connor, and Forrest Gump can't be filled completely with imbeciles. In fact, one person—who actually went off to college— is responsible for the name of this small Elmore County town. *Eclectic* means, basically, an assortment picked from a variety of styles. Apparently, one man came back from school talking about his eclectic course of study. Folks not used to such fancy book-larnin' seized on the word *eclectic* and decided it would make a nice name for the community.

But wait, there's more! It turns out that, perhaps, the folks of this town *were*, in fact, not very bright. A competing story about the origin of the town's name suggests that it was supposed to be *Electric*, suggesting the exciting growth expected in the community. Maps from the nineteenth century call the town *Electric*. Consequently, some a-hole who can't spell may accidentally have named the town *Eclectic*.

Nowadays Eclectic bills itself as "the star of Elmore County," which is akin to calling yourself "King Shit on Piss Island," but at least the folks in the community can claim a distinctive name. ↗

WHERE IS ECLECTIC?

Eclectic is in Elmore County, Alabama, not far from Montgomery.

WHY IS IT CALLED ECLECTIC?

Some suggest it was named for a man who went to college and came back talking about his *eclectic* curriculum. Others suggest the name was supposed to be *Electric*.

WHAT DO YOU NEED TO KNOW ABOUT ECLECTIC?

It's the star of Elmore County, Alabama.

EEK,
ALASKA

Eek! Help! We're in (gulp) Alaska! Get us the fuck out of here! What if we, like, see Sarah Palin or Russia or something? No wonder there's a freaking town in Alaska named Eek. It's what folks say, you know, when they're absolutely terrified of something that, well, is not really all that significant. Alaska may be the largest state of the union by size, but it's not exactly bursting at the seams with people. It's . . .well . . . not very significant. So, Eek!

Eek owes its name to native Alaskans, perhaps horrified at the thought that their land mass would, one day, be home to a bridge to nowhere. Of course, the "official" reason the community is named Eek is that "eek" is a native Alaskan word for "two eyes." What are the "two eyes" in question? Who knows? It's Alaska. Perhaps it refers to the entire population of the town. It's not a big place, after all. The population's minuscule, and the town is only about one square mile.

Still, the folks in Eek spend their days doing things folks throughout Alaska do: They wait for the sun to rise. They wait for the sun to set. They count snowflakes. They try desperately to fill countless boring hours, waiting only for the day that death will release them from living in a godforsaken town in a godforsaken state. Eek, indeed! ↗

> ### EEK! WHERE IS THIS PLACE?
> Eek is a small town near Bethel. Where's Bethel? Who knows? It's somewhere in Alaska.

> ### HOW DID EEK GET ITS NAME?
> *Eek* is a native Alaskan word that means "two eyes."

> ### WHAT DO YOU NEED TO KNOW ABOUT EEK?
> It's a very, very small place.

EFFIN,
IRELAND

Metalheads of the world unite. We have found your kingdom! It's true! The effin' tastiest frikkin' place in the whole world is in Ireland. It's totally near that effin' place you get dirty rhymes from, Limerick. How frikkin' cool is that?

Effin—used sometimes in place of the word *fucking*, by say, teenagers who are afraid to get into trouble or by Christians who don't want to use words that Jesus is purported to hate—is a town in Ireland. How in the world did it get its effin' name, you ask?

Effin is the Anglicized version of an Irish saint named *Eimhin*. No, this guy isn't as famous as St. Nicholas, St. Valentine, or even St. Vitus, but he was an honest-to-God real-life saint, who lived in the sixth century. Modern scholars believe he was the author of a massive biography of Ireland's patron saint, Patrick, the one known and celebrated the world over for giving us one more reason to get good and ripped on March 17.

Most Effin folks in Ireland spend their Effin time just getting through their Effin pathetic lives, going to their Effin schools, playing online solitaire at their Effin jobs, occasionally grabbing a pint or two at the Effin pub. These folks know how to Effin live. ↗

WHERE IS THIS EFFIN PLACE?

Effin is a small community in County Limerick, which gave its name to dirty poems.

HOW IN THE EFFIN WORLD DID IT GET ITS NAME?

Effin is the Anglicization of the name of an Irish saint, *Eimhin*.

WHAT DO YOU EFFIN NEED TO KNOW ABOUT EFFIN?

Its name sounds like a euphemism for the word *fucking*.

EIGHTY FOUR,
PENNSYLVANIA

The first question is: Where's the hyphen? Surely, even folks in rural Pennsylvania know that *eighty-four* contains a hyphen, right? So, why does Eighty Four, PA lack a hyphen?

Then, as you're pondering *that* question, you come up with one that is even more pressing: Why the hell is this town named after such a random number? Sure, Fifty-Six (note the hyphen, Pennsylvania!) was already taken by Arkansas (see page 76), but Eighty Four? WTF?

Theories regarding the town name's origin abound. One states that Eighty Four was given that name to honor Grover Cleveland's 1884 election to the presidency of the United States.

Another hypothesis is that the town was named for its mile marker along the Baltimore and Ohio Railroad. And still another claims the name was randomly chosen by a postmaster, after the town's post office was completed in 1884.

However its nondescript name came to be, the town is famous for one thing: It is the world headquarters of 84 Lumber, which started in the community. It's true! This not-quite-as-popular-as-Home-Depot hardware mega-store started in the community and, obviously, took its name from its hometown.

So, there you have it: Eighty Four, Pennsylvania. Now, listen, morons . . . about that hyphen . . . . ⤴

WHERE IS EIGHTY FOUR?

The town is about twenty-five miles from Pittsburgh and right smack dab in the middle of freaking nowhere.

WHY IS IT CALLED EIGHTY FOUR?

Most likely, Eighty Four got its name because the town was founded in 1884 and because the guy who named it lacked imagination.

WHAT DO YOU NEED TO KNOW ABOUT EIGHTY FOUR?

The sort-of famous 84 Lumber company started in Eighty Four, Pennsylvania.

ENIGMA,
GEORGIA

In its early days, the town-that-would-be-Enigma considered two names: Lax and Enigma. Now, these are both poor choices, in my opinion. *Lax* means, basically, "lazy," and *enigma* means "riddle." Both of these names completely suck.

You want a name for a town that will evoke strength, prosperity, security . . . shit, even conjuring up a sense of fun will do. But *Enigma*? That's like saying, "Well goddamn, we don't know what to call it, and we don't care what to call it, and Fagus (see page 75) is already taken."

Town founder, John Ball, decided around 1876 that his settlement needed a real name. Unofficially, the community was named Gunn and Weston, for reasons now lost to history.

Ball and other town residents came up (God knows how or why) with Lax and Enigma. If you can believe it, some other dipshit town nearby already was named Lax. So, Enigma it became.

Enigma is a quiet place with few businesses and, well, not much mystery. About the only thing that brings people to town is its annual Fourth of July celebration, at which Miss Enigma Firecracker (!!) is crowned. At least the town's name helps students learn big words like *enigma*. ↗

IT IS A RIDDLE . . .
Enigma is in Berrien County, not far from the Florida border.

WRAPPED IN A MYSTERY . . .
Enigma was, if you can believe it, the town's popular choice for a name. Perhaps it came from an inability to reach consensus on a more legitimate name.

INSIDE AN ENIGMA . . .
Enigma also considered the name *Lax*, which means "lazy." WTF?

EUREN,
WISCONSIN

For the record, we believe it is a wonderful tribute to name one's community after a foreign town that has meaning for locals. Since Wisconsin was settled largely by Germans, it's only fitting that one small town near Green Bay chose for itself the name of a small town in Germany. There's just one problem: The name sounds like the product that results from taking a piss.

Granted, the folks in Euren can call their town whatever they damn well please. And perhaps they are proud to be Eurenites? Eurenians? Euren specimens? For all we know, they are planning to secede from Wisconsin and start their own Euren nation.

But for the rest of us, non-Euranians, the name *Euren* is inherently funny. Think of it. Folks drive Euren cars, buy meat at the Euren butcher, and—grossest of all—down a few at Euren bars.

Of course, maybe the folks in this small town could turn their name from a bane to a boon. You know: "Welcome, Euren (read: You're in) Wisconsin's Sweetest Town!" Or, "Euren Luck! You've Come to Euren!" On second thought . . . nah. Any way you slice Euren, it's still a name with unpleasant associations. ↗

WHERE IS EUREN?
You will find it stored in your bladder.

WHY IS IT NAMED FOR PISS?
Euren takes its name from a German town of the same name. In German, the word means "your."

WHAT DO YOU NEED TO KNOW ABOUT EUREN?
Doing it publicly will get you arrested.

FAGUS,
MISSOURI

Is it any wonder Latin is a dead language? It's tough to learn, only dickheads like lawyers ever use it, and it's responsible for making a town in southern Missouri sound like it was named after gay people . . . not that there's anything wrong with that.

The lumber-rich community near the Arkansas border was founded by William Barron, who named it after the Latin word for "beech tree." Apparently, Barron named his town before he knew there actually *were* beech trees in it, in honor of his favorite trees back home. So, you can, in fact, find a fagus or two around.

Oh, and if you live in the area and don't particularly want to be known as a Fagut? Fagite? Fagustonian? then keep one thing in mind: It beats being called a Meatslapper. Before gaining the name *Fagus*, the community was known as *Slapout* because the local store was always "slap out of meat." ↗

DON'T BE SUCH A FAGUS.

Fagus is in Butler County, Missouri, near the Arkansas border.

WHO *IS* THIS FAGUS?

Fagus was named by town founder, William Barron, after the Latin word for beech tree.

NOT THAT THERE'S ANYTHING WRONG WITH THAT . . .

Fagus was once known as *Slapout*, as in "slap out of meat." It's true!

FIFTY-SIX,
ARKANSAS

Everyone wants to be number one. Who wants to be number two? That's a euphemism for shit, right? Once you get past one, you don't want to find yourself on any list of "bests" unless, say, it's the "best lover in the universe" or something.

That brings us to Fifty-Six, Arkansas. That, friends, is a pretty random number. How, you might ask, did this small community of some 165 people gain its name? The answer is that the preferred name was taken.

Yes. Sad but true, when names for the community were kicked around, everyone fawned over Pleasant Hill. It has a nice ring to it. It sounds like just the place where one could settle down, marry a toothless first cousin, and keep her barefoot and pregnant. Alas, a Pleasant Hill already existed in Arkansas. Apparently, after that, nobody really gave a rat's ass about the name of their community.

They opted for plan B, which was simply to name the town after the local school district, which happened to be fifty-six. This is what ambivalence will do for you . . . give you an awful name that means, basically, absolutely nothing. ↗

SCREW FIFTY-SIX. IS THERE ONE GOOD REASON I SHOULD CARE WHERE THIS PLACE IS?

Fifty-Six, Arkansas is in Stone County, near the northern border of the state.

I'M GONNA CRY FIFTY-SIX TEARS IF I DON'T KNOW WHY THIS PLACE HAS THIS NAME.

Fifty-Six is the number for the local school district.

WHAT DO YOU NEED TO KNOW ABOUT FIFTY-SIX, ARKANSAS?

You may be surprised to learn that there actually *are* fifty-six or more school districts in Arkansas.

FINGRINGHOE,
ENGLAND

How much does it cost if one merely wants to finger a ho? Only one town in the world knows the answer to this question with anything approaching certainty: Fingringhoe, England.

Fingringhoe has existed since Roman times, but the name is only about a thousand years old. Some believe the land was first settled by a man named Fingringas, and the current name derives from him.

Others believe the word comes from a mishmash of Old English that means "finger," as in "finger of land." Fingringhoe is a finger of land that helps to divert the River Colne in an eastward direction.

When not fing'ring hoes, Fingringhoe-ites? Fingringhoe-isans? spend their time at the Fingringhoe Wick Nature Preserve looking at salt marshes. Or perhaps they watch the tourists take pictures of all the hoes or of the town's traditional red telephone box.

Come to think of it (no pun intended), you might as well spend all your time there Fingringhoe. There's just not a whole hell of a lot else to do, and the hoes probably don't charge all that much for the act. ↗

WHERE IS FINGRINGHOE?

Fingringhoe is five miles from Colchester, a fairly large town in England's County Essex.

WHY IS IT NAMED FOR FINGERING HOES?

Fingringhoe might have been named for the man who first settled the land. Or it could be related to an Old English word for "finger" since the town forms a finger of land that diverts a river.

WHAT DO YOU NEED TO KNOW ABOUT FINGRINGHOE?

Prices may vary, depending on location and duration.

FISHKILL,
NEW YORK

PETA be damned! The organization that cares more about animals than it cares about people tried its best to cause this small, lower New York State town to change its name to something less offensive to fish and to fish-lovers.

The town said, in essence, "Suck it." Fishkill was founded by the Dutch. In Dutch, *kill* means "river" or "creek." So, the town's name simply means "Fish Creek." What's wrong with that? Presumably, there *are* fish in local creeks. Truth in advertising, baby!

In 1996, PETA didn't see it that way. The agency, brilliant and on-point as usual, decided the town should rename itself Fishsave. No shit! You can't make up stuff like this! Needless to say, the folks in Fishkill were used to being, well, the folks of Fishkill. And, just to reassert a point, *the name has nothing to do with killing fish.*

Sure, the name sounds animal unfriendly, and, to be honest, if the town were named Cutepuppykill or Adorablekittenkill then PETA might—just might, mind you—have a point.

But fish are not cuddly creatures. And *Fishkill*, while not the most pleasant name, has nothing to do with fish kills. If the town chooses to change its name it should be because it has found a better one. But, alas, Newfoundland already has claimed the town name "Dildo" (see page 60). ↗

WHERE CAN I GO TO KILL WILDLIFE?

Fishkill is north of New York City . . . far enough north not to be filled with the annoying brand of New Yorkers.

WHY IS IT NAMED AFTER MURDERING FISH?

Fishkill was settled by the Dutch. In Dutch, *kill* means "river" or "creek."

WHAT DO YOU NEED TO KNOW ABOUT FISHKILL?

PETA tried to get the town to rename itself *Fishsave*.

FLUSHING,
NETHERLANDS

Just because Holland doesn't have much more to offer than tulips, legal hookers, and tons of legal weed . . . God, what are we saying? This place is paradise on Earth. We'll even tiptoe through the tulips to get to that weed and those hookers!

Oh, well, back to the initial concept. Just because there's not a lot to Holland doesn't mean you should flush the whole damn thing down the toilet. It's a real country, after all, with lots of dykes. And who wouldn't want to see all those dykes together? Beautiful! In so many words: There's just no excuse for naming a major port in the Netherlands *Flushing*. It suggests flushing something down, like a dead goldfish or post–Taco Bell turds. Flushing? Well, we never!

It turns out that, in fact, *Flushing* is the English name of the town. The Dutch name is *Vlissingen*, which means "bottle." Two stories exist to explain this odd choice of a name. In one tale, St. Willibrord landed in the community in the seventh century, carrying a bottle. He used the water in the bottle to feed beggars, and—miraculously—the bottle's contents never depleted. Perhaps it was just backwash? The other story is that a ferry that once was used in the area had a bottle on its sign. The ferry house was called *het veer aan de Flesse*, which means "the ferry at the bottle."

However the name came to be, this port city now bears a name that puts one in mind of flushing unwanted things—dead pets, waste products, that no-longer-legal weed—down the toilet. ↗

WHERE IS ALL THIS FLUSHING HAPPENING?

Flushing is in south-western Holland.

WHY IS IT NAMED *FLUSHING*?

Two stories exist to explain the name. Both are concerned with the word *bottle*, which is, basically, what Flushing's Dutch name, *Vlissingen*, means.

WHAT DO YOU NEED TO KNOW ABOUT FLUSHING?

The town in New York is named for the Dutch city.

THE FOOL KILLER,
NEW HAMPSHIRE

Clearly, God did not intend for people to climb tall mountains. He expects them to sit motionless in front of televisions for hours. Want proof? Sedentary lifestyles kill way more people than death from exposure or hypothermia atop craggy peaks. But that doesn't stop New Hampshire's Fool Killer from trying.

Here's the problem . . . a popular climb for White Mountain hikers is Mount Tripyramid, so called because it has three peaks. From certain vantage points, hikers can start up what they think is part of Tripyramid and discover they're actually on a 3,500-foot peak separated from Tripyramid by a long valley and a ridge. D'oh! Dumb ass! Next time, ask for directions, moron.

The Fool Killer is aptly named because some assholes consider themselves immortal and try hiking the whole damn thing anyway, even though they only have enough provisions for a shorter climb. To paraphrase Spinal Tap: There's a fine line between stupid and clever. Some fools in New Hampshire don't live to cross that line. ⬈

YO, FOOL, WHERE IS THIS PLACE?

The Fool Killer is a 3,491-foot peak in New Hampshire's White Mountains. Some schmucks like you climb the damn thing by mistake.

HOW DID IT GET SUCH A FOOLISH NAME?

Due to the schmucks referenced above.

YO, FOOL, WHAT DO I NEED TO KNOW ABOUT IT?

Make sure you intend to climb it, dumb ass.

FREAK LAKE,
ALASKA

There's no better place to freak out than in Alaska. It's home to moose hunters, sled dogs, midnight sun, and presidential wannabes who think they have foreign policy experience based on the state's proximity to Russia.

Is it any wonder, then, that you will find Freak Lake in such a place? Did it get its name because prescient explorers knew that, one day, Sarah Palin would call the state home? Did it get its name because it gives rise to monsters and/or Sasquatches bent on terrorizing unwitting Iditarod contestants?

No. In fact, Freak Lake got its name arbitrarily. It's true! According to the United States Board on Geographic Names, Freak Lake was a random word starting with "F" used for tactical purposes during World War II. The name "Freak Lake" officially showed up on Army documents in 1953.

So, there you go. Freaks like you . . . folks who just like to get freaky . . . ladies who want to get their freak on. All of you have a place to call your own. And why not be *really* freaky and try skinny dipping in Freak Lake? No, don't. It's found among the Aleutian Islands, and the water is, surely, cold enough to freeze your balls off. ↗

> **WHERE THE FREAK IS THIS LAKE?**
> Freak Lake is found on one of the Aleutian Islands in Alaska.

> **WHY IS IT SO FREAKY?**
> *Freak* was just a random word that starts with "F" used by the military for mapping purposes.

> **WHAT DO YOU NEED TO KNOW ABOUT FREAK LAKE?**
> It's cold enough to freeze one's naughty bits right off.

FRENCH LICK,
INDIANA

No, dickwad, a French Lick isn't something you pay extra for when you're trawling the local red light district, it's basketball great Larry Bird's hometown!

Before its name resembled a venereal disease or sexual activity, French Lick was the site of a French trading post near a salt lick and a spring. For many years, the community was called Salt Spring. Lost to history is the name of the genius who changed harmless-sounding "Salt Spring" to "French Lick."

For most of its existence, French Lick was a spa town that attracted the likes of gangster Al Capone and Irving Berlin to its quasi-legal casinos, which ultimately closed. In response to Indiana's recent legalization of casino gambling, the French Lick Resort Casino opened in 2007, bringing back the glory days of gambling, spa treatments, and craigslist.com adult services. ↗

WHERE CAN I GET A FRENCH LICK?

Give me a hundred bucks, and I'll send you to the right place.

WHY FRENCH LICK?

The area was once a French trading post near a salt lick.

WHAT DO I NEED TO KNOW ABOUT FRENCH LICK?

It's a spa/casino city and the hometown of NBA great, Larry Bird.

FUCKING,
AUSTRIA

Fuckers have lived in Austria for nearly a thousand years, greeting their Fucking neighbors, purchasing their Fucking groceries, sending their Fucking kids to Fucking schools. If there's any spot on the planet where even *you* are sure to see some Fucking, it's right here.

A man with the last name *Focko* moved to the area in the sixth century. When it came time to put the town he founded on the map, government officials used a variation of his name, added an "ing" to it—denoting "place of Focko's people"—and, thus, Fucking was born. Even though the town is full of Fucking Fuckers, its population is just over one hundred.

Fucking is a peaceful place, though town officials have been plagued for generations by fuckers—with a lower-case "f"—stealing the Fucking sign at the Fucking village limits. As a result, the signs were made theft-proof in 2005. Or at least that appears to be the theory behind placing them on really heavy things that are hard to steal.

Why doesn't the village just change its name to something less titillating? Locals contend that they've been Fuckers for a thousand years. Why should they stop Fucking now? ↗

WHERE THE FUCK IS IT?

Fucking, Austria, is twenty miles from Salzburg and close to the German border. You can practically see Fuckers from the Rhineland.

HOW THE FUCK DID IT GET ITS NAME?

Long, long ago, the Focko family moved to the area. Over time, the name mutated slightly, making descendants part of the Fuck family. The "-ing" denotes "place of Focko's (or Fuck's) people."

WHAT THE FUCK DO YOU NEED TO KNOW ABOUT FUCKING?

People have attempted to steal the village sign for years. Eventually, Fuckers got so pissed off that they tried to make the Fucking signs theft-proof.

FUKUYMAMA,
JAPAN

Say the name of one town in Japan to most Americans, and you'll get your ass kicked double quick. In fact, actually *do* try this at home. Go up to a stranger in an unfamiliar neighborhood and say, "Fukuymama." Then, see if your ass gets kicked. If it does, don't blame us because only an idiot would take that dare.

Of course, *Fukuymama* probably isn't actually pronounced "fuck you mama," but that's what it looks like to English speakers and, especially, to ugly Americans who don't give a rat's ass how other countries pronounce stuff since, obviously, it should be pronounced the way *we* think it should be pronounced.

Fukuymama is a town near Hiroshima (yes, *that* Hiroshima) located on the Ashida River. The city is small by Japanese standards, having only 500,000 people packed like sardines in hermetic tin cans.

For the Japanese, the city is most famous for its annual rose festival, and for English-speakers, it's most famous for having a name that looks like an insult to one's sainted mama. In fact, *fukuymama* is a Japanese word that refers to the island nation's famous Mt. Fuji. It means "mountain of wind."

So, the next time you get drunk and say something inappropriate about someone else's mama, just smile, shake your head in an apologetic way and tell your imminent ass-kicker that you were simply trying to engage him in a conversation about a small Japanese city. You'll still get your ass kicked, but at least you'll get to feel smart for a moment beforehand. ➚

WHERE IS FUKUYMAMA?

What did you say, motherfucker? Oh. It's near Hiroshima.

WHY IS IT NAMED FUKYMAMA?

Fukuymama means "mountain of wind," and it's a Japanese word for "Mt. Fuji."

WHAT DO YOU NEED TO KNOW ABOUT FUKUYMAMA?

The city was bombed by conventional weapons just after Hiroshima was hit by a nuclear bomb.

GAY AND LESBIAN KINGDOM

OF THE CORAL SEA ISLANDS

Oh my God! Do you know where, just, the most *fabulous* place on Earth can be found? No, it's not 'Frisco. It's not gay marriage–friendly Vermont. It's found among the Coral Sea Islands, off the coast of Australia. Isn't that so completely *fabulous*?!?

Actually, the Gay and Lesbian Kingdom of the Coral Sea Islands isn't very fah-boo just yet. It's uninhabited.

The kingdom is a micronation, the term given to places that sort of act like nations but that aren't, in fact, recognized as political entities by any other countries. Like other micronations, the Gay and Lesbian Kingdom of the Coral Sea Islands makes money by printing postage stamps. Unlike other micronations, the Gay and Lesbian Kingdom's stamps are *fabulous*, featuring the "nation's" beautiful rainbow flag.

How did such a place come to be? The "kingdom" was founded in 2004 by a group of gay-rights activists protesting a same-sex marriage ban by the Australian parliament. One of the group's members, Dale Anderson, declared himself the micronation's first emperor, Dale I.

So, if you're looking for a place to enjoy Judy Garland films and Barbra Streisand albums proudly and without shame, then just find Queensland, Australia (yes, seriously), then head out to sea. ➜

WHERE IS THIS *FABULOUS* PLACE?

The Coral Sea Islands are a bunch of mostly uninhabited islands off the coast of Queensland, Australia. One of these islands is home to this fabulous micronation.

WHY DOES IT EXIST?

The Gay and Lesbian Kingdom of the Coral Sea Islands was founded in 2004 to protest the Australian parliament's decision to ban same-sex marriage.

OOH, WHAT DO YOU NEED TO KNOW ABOUT THIS *FABULOUS* PLACE?

The "nation" makes its money by selling stamps and by catering the occasional gay fisherman/fisherwoman/fisher-trans-gendered-human-being.

GAY,
MICHIGAN

There is one fabulous place in Michigan guaranteed to be just bursting with Gay pride. Yep, the annual Gay Parade, held on the Fourth of July, attracts people from throughout the region, and the town's only thriving business is the Gay Bar.

Gay, Michigan, is named for town founder, Joseph E. Gay. At one time, it was home to thriving mining-related industries; today, Gay is proudly represented by the Gay Bar . . . perhaps the world's only Gay Bar that is not, in fact, a "gay bar." Rather, it is named for the town and its founder.

The bar is located in what once was the home of a bigwig in Joseph Gay's Mohawk Mining Company. Owners have included the Lodges and the Dicks (no joke). The Gay Bar proudly sells all sorts of fabulous Gay merchandise, including Gay Bar thongs for the ladies!

The old mining operations are gone, but in this corner of Michigan's upper peninsula, the Gay times remain. ↗

> **THAT'S SO GAY!**

Gay is in Michigan's least populous county. Perhaps there will be more people there one day, if attitudes about Gay marriage ever change.

> **GAY PRIDE**

Gay is named for town founder and mining executive, Joseph E. Gay.

> **WHAT'S SO GAY ABOUT IT?**

The Gay Bar, a place with a sense of humor, is the town's only real business. It is not a "gay bar," though gay people would not be unwelcome.

GEORGE,
WASHINGTON

Some cities actually have a sense of humor. Case in point: George, Washington. The town began as an irrigation district, and by the early 1950s, the resulting agricultural boom made it necessary to situate a town there.

The Bureau of Land Management put aside a few hundred acres and opened the land up for bids. The winning bidder would be in charge of creating a new metropolis. When the bidding was over, no one, it seemed, was interested in starting a new town.

Well, that's not entirely true. There was *one* bid, that of local pharmacist, Charlie Brown (seriously). Brown, with a little help, designed a town and its governmental structure. Then, when it came time to name the place, he had a brainstorm: Name it *George*, as a humorous way to honor the nation's first president, George Washington.

The town's website declares that George is "the only city in the nation named after the full name of a president." And the George Washington fun doesn't end there. Every year, the city goes absolutely batshit for Independence Day, offering the "world's largest cherry pie" and the "everything-you-could-possible [*sic*]-hope for" July 4th celebration.

Wow! What's not to like? Well . . . there's the fact that the town is, basically, in the middle of nowhere and that, after a while, all the George Washington jokes would probably make one angry enough to imitate Washington and start wielding an axe. ↗

BY GEORGE!

George is in Grant County, right about in the middle of the state.

WHY IS IT NAMED GEORGE, WASHINGTON?

Because of the first president, dumb ass.

WHAT DO YOU NEED TO KNOW ABOUT GEORGE, WASHINGTON?

It was founded by Charlie Brown. Good grief.

GLASSCOCK COUNTY,
TEXAS

Does it come as any surprise to find that this is the most Republican county in the entire United States? After all, *glass* suggests something brittle and potentially harmful. *Cock* suggests a dick, as in a person who acts like a douche. Put the words together, and you have a brittle, dangerous penis.

In 2000, 93 percent of the people in this Texas county voted for the Republican presidential ticket. So, we have Glasscock to thank for eight years of rule by a brittle, dangerous penis . . . and that other guy, Bush, who worked for him.

The county was named for George Washington Glasscock, a man who managed to do quite a bit despite having an embarrassing name. He was an acquaintance of Abraham Lincoln, fought with him in the Black Hawk War, served Texas in the state legislature, opened the first flour mill in west Texas, and even found time to manage the state's lunatic asylum. All of that, while possessing a glass cock. Imagine!

Today, Glasscock County is best known for being solid Red. So, blame *them* for putting Dick Cheney in charge. In addition, the town is on top of the Spraberry Trend, the third-largest oil field in the United States. So, visit Glasscock today. Just beware of brittle, dangerous penises. ↗

WHERE IS GLASSCOCK?

It's pretty near the heel of the Texas "boot." The county seat is Garden City.

WHY IS IT NAMED FOR A BRITTLE, DANGEROUS PENIS?

The county was named for early Texas settler, George Washington Glasscock.

WHAT DO YOU NEED TO KNOW ABOUT GLASSCOCK?

Remove your Obama sticker before driving through, unless you just want to die.

GNAW BONE,
INDIANA

Who knew that folks in the self-proclaimed "Flea Market Capital of the World" were such kinky freaks? There you are, minding your own business as you drive down state highway 46, listening to something shitty on the radio, sexting while driving, the usual. Oh, there's Nashville. You've heard there's some good pickin's in Columbus.

Then, suddenly . . . *Gnaw Bone*?!? What possessed perfectly normal folks in the center of America's heartland to name a town after such a thing? You drive on a little bit faster, your heart racing along with your engine.

No one really knows why this small, unincorporated community is named Gnaw Bone. The most likely explanation is that it is an "Americanization" of *Narbonne*, the name of a French city, perhaps the one from which early Indiana settlers arrived.

Another theory suggests that a man was in search of an old friend and asked a local for help locating the long-lost buddy. Supposedly, the stranger was told that his friend had been seen across the way "a gnawin' on a bone." Not very fucking likely, but you never know.

Nowadays, Gnaw Bone and other towns in this part of Indiana are best known for flea markets. Chances are, at least some of them sell T-shirts that will allow you to brag to all your friends that you like Gnaw Bone. And you know you do, you kinky freak, you. ↗

> **GNAW ON THIS.**
>
> Gnaw Bone is a sparsely populated community in sparsely populated Brown County, Indiana.

> **EAT IT, LICK IT, GNAW IT.**
>
> Gnaw Bone probably is the mispronunciation of *Narbonne*, a French city apparently appreciated by early settlers to the region.

> **AW, GO GNAW ON A BONE.**
>
> Gnaw Bone is smack dab in the middle of the "Flea Market Capital of the World."

GOFUKU,
JAPAN

We've got some advice for you. Head to Japan, take an elevator to the top of the Gofuku Tower, gofukuself, and then jump off. Nah, just kidding . . . well, about the killing yourself part. Go ahead and climb the tower, but don't jump off. Just gofukuself.

In fact, while you're in this exotic spot, with its campus of the University of Toyama and its park, you will find all kinds of places to gofukuself. There's the Gofuku Park, the aforementioned Gofuku Tower, and probably all sorts of Gofuku streets. Knock yourself out!

In truth, though we'd be fine if you did, in fact, decide to gofukuself, the name of this Japanese city is a little misleading. In English, *gofuku* sounds like the sort of insult you hear every Saturday night at that loser singles bar. In Japanese, *gofuku* is not rude at all. Translated into English the word means something like "draperies" or "dry goods," such as sheets, linens, that sort of thing.

Nonetheless, the city has become somewhat infamous because its name is just so darn hilarious in English. Countless websites tout the community as having one of the "rudest" names in the world. The fine folks at the research-oriented university must be so goddamn proud. ↗

WHERE IS GOFUKU?

It's in Japan, genius. Where else?

WHY IS IT NAMED *GOFUKU*?

Because, in Japanese, the word means "draperies" or "dry goods." Once upon a time, the city must have specialized in such items.

WHAT DO YOU NEED TO KNOW ABOUT GOFUKU?

It contains a plethora of places at which to gofukuself.

GREAT SNORING,
ENGLAND

England has a reputation for being, well, boring. You know: staid, bland, insipid. But there *are* some exciting places. London swings . . . or at least it did, for a while in the 1960s. Soccer (sorry Brits . . . football only exists in America) games in Manchester are really just an excuse for fighting.

The rest of the country is, well, as boring as a plate of two-day-old faggots and beans. But of all the boring spots in the Mother Country, one surely wins the boredom contest: Great Snoring.

Do you need proof? First off, Great Snoring is in the middle of fucking nowhere. In England, *rural village* can be translated as: "at least a hundred miles from anything that will remind you you're in the twenty-first century and probably filled with lovely, lovely sheep." Secondly, the town's population has dropped from 600 to 200 over the last 150 years, as people have woken up to the incessant boredom of their village.

Snoring was named during Saxon times for a man named Snear. Over time, it became Snoring. Why is it "great"? Because, if you can believe it, there's actually a Little Snoring nearby, and *it's* the region's hot spot. People from Great Snoring go to Little Snoring to do their shopping and have something amounting to a night on the town. Most likely, it sucks completely to live in *either* place. ➐

WHERE (SNORE) IS GREAT SNORING?

Great Snoring is on the banks of the River Stiffkey, in North Norfolk.

WHY IS IT (SNORE) NAMED *GREAT SNORING*?

The town was named for a man named Snear, and, over time, "snear" became "snoring." It's "great" because Little Snoring is two miles down the lane.

WHAT DO YOU NEED TO (SNORE) KNOW ABOUT GREAT SNORING?

It's one of the most boring places in England, which makes it one of the most boring spots in the entire world!

GRIPE,
ARIZONA

The weather? It sucks. Your relationship? It's nonexistent, or it sucks. Your house? Sucks? Your car? Sucks. Your job? Jesus, don't get us started! But, you see, it's okay to complain. It beats the alternative: going out of your everloving mind and winding up in a loony bin or in a police lineup.

One community, out in the middle of the Arizona desert, has raised griping to an art form. In fact, they're so proud of their ability to bitch at length that they've actually named their community *Gripe*.

And it's not like *Gripe* is some bizarre Anglicization of a Native American word that means, "godforsaken spot in the middle of the fucking desert," or something. No! The town *actually* is named for griping.

Anyone who has driven through portions of the Desert Southwest knows that agricultural stations are a way of life. These agricultural stations keep exotic insects and plant viruses from getting into farmland, but they also cause you to lose time on your travels. That's why folks who lived near one of these stations griped and complained about it so much that they decided to name their community Gripe. It's true!

So, you think *you* know how to bitch, moan, and complain? Don't talk to us unless you're willing to name one of your children Bitch, Moan, Complain, or Gripe. ↗

WHERE IS GRIPE?

Gripe is some 100 miles from Tucson and some 30 miles from the New Mexico border.

WHY IS IT NAMED *GRIPE*?

Folks in the area complained so much about a local agricultural station that they opted to call their community Gripe.

WHAT DO YOU NEED TO KNOW ABOUT GRIPE?

It seems to us that living in the middle of nowhere in the godforsaken desert would be a much greater gripe.

GROSS,
NEBRASKA

New York City and other such metropolises may be able to boast heaps of garbage, crime, and many instances of public urination. But they have no claim to be America's most disgusting city. No, the village that can claim such laurels is in Nebraska.

Gross, Nebraska, is, in truth, named for an early postmaster named B.B. Gross. It's not gross at all, but the town lacks a good PR guy. As of the 2000 census, Gross could claim only five (five!) residents. The sign welcoming visitors to the city only credits the town with three (three!) people.

Perhaps newcomers are frightened away by the village's name, evocative of decay, shit, vomit, maggots, and all sorts of other unpleasant things.

Or, maybe, just maybe, the one family that lives in Gross is comprised of total assholes. You can always visit and find out for yourself. ➚

SHEESH, WHAT'S THAT SMELL?

It's Gross! Gross, Nebraska is in Boyd County, near the state's border with South Dakota.

EWWW, GROSS!

Gross was named for an early postmaster, B. B. Gross.

YOU ARE, LIKE, SO TOTALLY GROSS!

Gross features an inn that carries the slogan, "Lifestyles of the Poor and Unknown."

HAPPY,
TEXAS

Hey, asshole, cheer up! You could be working in a Chinese sweatshop making sweat socks for major American retailers. Or you could be working as a nursing assistant in an old-folk's home, spending your time getting paid peanuts to wipe up the various bodily fluids and solids of the elderly.

Even if you *are* a CNA, there's a place you can visit that's guaranteed to make you smile. Yep. Happy, Texas, bills itself as "The Town without a Frown." Nothing short of a shot of nitrous is more likely to give you a super case of the jollies.

Happy originally was named "Happy Draw" because early cowpokes were so thrilled to find a place with a water supply in the area. Since that time, Happy has remained, shit-eating grin firmly in place, at the base of the Texas panhandle.

For a place with fewer than 700 people, Happy has several claims to fame. A 1999 film titled *Happy, Texas* was supposed to take place in town, though it actually was filmed elsewhere. A character from the popular television series, *24*, hails from Happy. And Buddy Knox, who scored a big hit long ago with "Party Doll," is a Happy, Texas native.

So, turn that frown upside down and head for Happy. But bring that nitrous along . . . you know, just in case. ↗

> **WE'RE SO HAPPY!**
>
> Happy actually spreads itself between two counties, but it is considered part of metropolitan Amarillo.

> **HAPPY HAPPY JOY JOY!**
>
> Happy, Texas was named by cowboys, who were happy to find a water source there.

> **C'MON, GET HAPPY!**
>
> Happy bills itself as "The Town without a Frown." Its slogan was mentioned in a VISA credit card ad in the 1990s.

HARDWOOD,
OKLAHOMA

One must admire a town willing to name itself after not one, but TWO synonyms for an erection, boner, trouser tent, and Mr. Stiffy. Yep, the folks of Hard-(snicker)-wood-(snicker) have got guts . . . as well as an epidemic of morning wood.

Hardwood was named for the presence of hardwood trees in the area, but, shit fire, even back in the day wouldn't Hardwood settlers have had *some* idea of what they were doing? After all *hard-on* has meant "fat peter" since the mid-to-late nineteenth century. And *wood*, as in "fat peter," has probably been around at least that long.

Nowadays, the folks in town have plenty of opinions about the pros and cons of Hardwood. They take photos of Hardwood and post them online. They have hard-ons for civic pride. They get their meat at Hardwood grocery stores.

And if they're not careful, they may find themselves in need of trouser monsters. Oklahoma hardwoods have been heavily forested over the years. By 1956, only 15 percent of the state's hardwoods remained. Bottom line: The men of Oklahoma need to protect their Hardwood at all costs. ↗

WHERE CAN I FIND HARDWOOD?

Hardwood is in Coal County, not far from Hard On. Oh, wait. That's the community of *Harden*.

WHY IS IT NAMED FOR A BONER?

Actually, Hardwood is named for the presence of hardwood trees like oaks and elms.

WHAT DO I NEED TO KNOW ABOUT HARDWOOD?

It's like two, two, two erection synonyms in one.

HEADLESS CHICKEN FESTIVAL:
FRUITA, COLORADO

Some towns have festivals honoring their war dead. Others have festivals commemorating famous historical events. Fruita, Colorado has something way cooler: a festival honoring a headless chicken.

Mike was born like all other chickens, with his head intact. On the fateful morning of September 10, 1945, Mike's owner, Lloyd Olsen, went out to send Mike's spirit to its final reward and Mike's body to the dinner table. Olsen chopped off Mike's head with one blow.

It's not unusual for chickens to live without their heads for a short time, but Mike survived for eighteen months without a brain in his head—not quite as long as Paris Hilton, but a good long while, nonetheless.

Mike's will to live inspired those who paid a quarter to see him at sideshows across the country. Fed with an eyedropper, Mike not only lived, he grew to be a hefty eight pounds. Finally, death, as it must to all chickens, came to Mike, "The Headless Wonder Chicken."

Since 1999, folks in Fruita have chosen the third weekend in May to celebrate "Mike the Headless Chicken Day." As the festival's website proclaims, "Attending this fun, family event is a no brainer." Hey, anybody hungry for some KFC? ⤴

HEADLESS CHICKEN?!? WHERE THE HELL?

Fruita, Colorado, is near the Utah border and the Colorado city of Grand Junction.

HEADLESS CHICKEN?!? WHY THE HELL?

Mike the Headless Chicken survived for eighteen months without a head. What's not to celebrate?

HEADLESS CHICKEN?!? WHAT THE HELL?

Mike the Headless Chicken Day is too important to be celebrated in a single day. It takes place throughout the third weekend in May.

HEAD-SMASHED-IN BUFFALO JUMP,
CANADA

Hey, kids! Get in the car! We're taking you to a super-duper place! It's a United Nations Educational, Scientific, and Cultural Organization (UNESCO) World Heritage Site! It's in the foothills of the Rocky Mountains! It's in beautiful Alberta, Canada! Oh, what's its name? Um . . . well . . . it's Head-Smashed-In Buffalo Jump. Hey, kids, why are you crying?

This world heritage site once was used by the Blackfoot and other indigenous tribes as a way to kill buffalo, which the native people used for food, clothing, and tax write-offs. The Indians would round up buffalo and force them over a 30-foot cliff. The cause of death? The smashing-in of buffalo heads.

But, wait, kids! That's not how the site got its name. According to legend, one Blackfoot brave wanted to watch the buffalo fall, so he got underneath the cliff and waited. Oops! He didn't get out of the way fast enough, and his head was smashed in by a falling buffalo.

The cliff was such a great success that it was used for 6,000 years. When excavated in modern times, buffalo bones were found in a pile 30-feet deep. Indigenous people stopped using the Head-Smashed-In Buffalo Jump when, who else, white folks came to town and ruined everything. Now, it's a beautiful and bucolic spot, ruined only by a name that brings fear to the hearts of children . . . and PETA members. ↗

WHERE IS HEAD-SMASHED-IN BUFFALO JUMP?

You'll find it at the foothills of the Rocky Mountains, in Alberta, Canada.

WHY IS IT CALLED HEAD-SMASHED-IN BUFFALO JUMP?

An idiotic Blackfoot brave got his head smashed in by a falling buffalo. Yes, you'd have to be pretty fucking stupid not to get out of the way.

WHAT DO YOU NEED TO KNOW ABOUT HEAD-SMASHED-IN BUFFALO JUMP?

It's a UNESCO World Heritage Site that contains a museum devoted to Blackfoot culture.

HELL,
MICHIGAN

Satan sucks. His kingdom is, like, underground some-where and hot all the time and, in general, a pain in the ass. Who'd want to go there? Besides, you can find Hell closer to home. It's in Michigan.

The story goes that a workaholic and his shrew-ish wife helped put Hell on the map. George Reeves spent so much time at his mill and at his whiskey still that, when asked for his location, his wife would say that George had gone to Hell. The name stuck and became official in 1841.

The folks in Hell have a pretty good sense of humor, despite living in the middle of, well, Hell. Local stores allow you to buy "stuff from Hell," including T-shirts and baseball caps, as well as "Spe-cial Gift Baskets from Hell." Save 'em up and give 'em to ex-girlfriends! ↗

WHERE THE HELL IS IT?

Hell, Michigan, is about sixty miles from Detroit, the *actual* site of Hell on Earth.

HOW THE HELL DID IT GET ITS NAME?

Supposedly, when folks from the state came around to ask town founder George Reeves what to call his town he told them they could call it Hell for all he cared. In truth, the state thought *Hell* was softer than Reeves's actual response: *Fuck Off*.

WHAT THE HELL DO YOU NEED TO KNOW ABOUT IT?

Folks in Hell bank on selling souvenirs with their town's beloved name emblazoned thereon. Oh, and Satan sucks.

HOOKER,
OHIO

Not far from Columbus is a town filled with Hookers. Female ones. Male ones. Old ones. Young ones. Hookers as far as the eye can see, and the best part . . . they don't charge! Yep, you can interact with any of these Hookers absolutely free! Go ahead. Proposition away!

If you get slapped, don't blame us. We warned you that Hooker, Ohio, was named for Samuel Hooker, who settled this part of Fairfield County. All of the Hookers in his family begat more Hookers who begat more Hookers.

One imagines that, each year, hundreds of horny Ohio State University fraternity rejects head to this Columbus suburb with high hopes . . . only to find that the hookers are nowhere to be found. Then, there's nothing for them to do but get shitfaced—again—and spend the night flogging the dolphin.

Come to think of it, if the folks in Hooker were smart they'd just go ahead and get into the pay-for-sex biz. After all, Columbus free papers are chock full of prostitution advertisements, which lead to near-constant sting operations designed to put an end to the business.

Talk about hiding in plain sight! Hooker could just start using some slogan like "Friendly Hooker . . . Ready to Meet Your Every Need." And, *bam!*, just watch that money roll in to the community's coffers. Give us a kickback, will ya? ↗

WHERE CAN I FIND HOOKERS?

Hooker is in Fairfield County, Ohio. It's basically a suburb of Columbus, the state's capital and home to several colleges and universities, including Ohio State.

WHO ARE THESE HOOKERS?

Hooker was named for Samuel Hooker and his family, early settlers to the area.

WHAT DO I NEED TO KNOW ABOUT HOOKERS?

It's not wise to write them checks. Doing so caused one-time Ohio politician, Jerry Springer, to end his political career and start a television show that's the equivalent of a demolition derby in a trailer park.

HOPEULIKIT,
GEORGIA

A town's name can come from nearly anything: an offhand comment, a founder's ego, the Anglicization of a Native American word. Sometimes, a name can come from a local landmark or famous resident. And then, every once in a while, you'll find a place that was named for a shit-kickin' music venue.

During the swing era of the 1920s and 1930s, the Hopeulikit was a dance hall that attracted some of music's biggest names to an unincorporated community near Statesboro, Georgia. The music hall was such a big draw that folks in the area started to call the surrounding community Hopeulikit as well.

The dance hall fell on hard times and became a juke joint, favored by ruffians and hooligans, then became a liquor store, then burned down. But Hopeulikit, the town, remained. It's pretty much just a wide spot in the road, nothing much to like, but it may not even be that for much longer.

The state of Georgia has begun to remove the community's name from official maps. That sucks. Quick! Go down and grab a stray Hopeulikit sign while it's still around. Then put it up over your bed or something. ↗

WHAT'S THERE TO LIKE?

Hopeulikit is an unincorporated community in Bulloch County, Georgia, near Statesboro.

I HOPE YOU LIKE IT.

The community is named for a once-popular dance hall that burned down long ago.

WHAT'S *NOT* TO LIKE?

Being in the middle of fucking nowhere in Georgia.

HORNEYTOWN,
NORTH CAROLINA

Old folks in one placid corner of North Carolina's Forsyth County cackle at Viagra. They sneer at Cialis. And little wonder! Folks in the community have been in a constant state of arousal for well over 150 years. It's a wonder that any work gets done in Horneytown.

Horneytown has been stimulating snickers since what local (redneck) folks call the War of Northern Aggression. Around that time, the family that gave the town its name settled, and residents have been Horney ever since.

Apparently, all the folks in this section of the Tarheel State have a hard-on for sex. After all, Horneytown is within spitting distance (and just what are they spitting?) of Climax, Erect, and High Point. Brother, you've found your new home! ↗

WON'T YOU TAKE ME TO HORNEYTOWN?

Sure. It's in Forsyth County, North Carolina, very close to High Point.

HOW DID THE PLACE BECOME SUCH A HORNEYTOWN?

The Horney family settled there during the Civil War era. No incest jokes, please.

WHAT DO YOU NEED TO KNOW ABOUT HORNEYTOWN?

The local volunteer fire department does a thriving business selling "Horneytown VFD" T-shirts.

HOT COFFEE,
MISSISSIPPI

If you're a "caffiend," then you might consider high-tailing it to a small town in Mississippi. Sure, you might still have to endure the presence of folks who proudly claim to be descendants of Confederate generals, but until there's a community in the country named after Red Bull, your best bet for a town to meet your caffeine fix is Hot Coffee.

The Covington County village is named for a nineteenth-century inn that specialized in beaver pelts and squirrel brain soufflé. No, it had renowned coffee, numbnuts. The inn has gone to the Great Hotelier in the Sky, but Hot Coffee, the community, remains.

Oddly enough, however, it ain't easy to find a cup o' joe in this town. It's the only spot in the free world that does not contain a Starbucks, and it doesn't even have a no-name coffee house.

Why should it? Coffee houses are where beatniks and hippies congregate, and long hairs, to this day, are not welcome in Hot Coffee. Do you want proof? Just check out the sign in front of the community's market that warns, "No loud or vulgar music allowed."

That's right! Even if folks can't hear it, they don't want "vulgar" music stirring up Hot Coffee. You know what? If you're really in need of a java fix, you probably should stay the hell out of Mississippi altogether. Hell, even if you're *not* in need of a java fix, you should probably stay out of Mississippi altogether. ↗

WHERE IS HOT COFFEE?

It is in Covington County, far from a Starbucks.

WHY IS IT NAMED *HOT COFFEE*?

Because coffee fucking rocks! And because there was once an inn there that sold hot coffee.

WHAT DO YOU NEED TO KNOW ABOUT HOT COFFEE?

Internet chatter suggests that you cannot actually get a cup of coffee in the town! Bummer.

HOT SPOT,
KENTUCKY

The phrase *hot spot* suggests many things. You might picture a place at which you can surf the Internet for free on your laptop. You may think of the kind of "swinging hot spot" Joni Mitchell sang about in "Big Yellow Taxi."

Hell, you might even think of the clitoris or the G-spot. In fact, you're *most* likely to think of these particular "hot spots" because you would have to have a juvenile sense of humor in order to read a book like this.

But whatever crosses your mind, chances are you're *not* thinking of Kentucky coal fields. Yet, that's where you'll find Hot Spot.

Kentucky coal fields conjure mental images of grimy, overworked men who are just waiting to die from some rare form of lung cancer. You imagine eternally gray skies and a chewed-up landscape. Paradise, it ain't. Shit. Detroit would be preferable to *this*, and Detroit totally sucks.

So, how did a place like this become the nation's Hot Spot? Simple. It's called corporate fascism. Hot Spot was named for the Hot Spot Coal Company. Hot Spot was the piper that employed much of the town in its lung-cancer-inducing mines, so it called the tune; in fact, it named the tune after itself.

Forget Hot Spot, Kentucky. You're better off trying to figure out how to find the G-spot. ↗

WHERE IS HOT SPOT?

It's in the last place you'd think to find it: Kentucky coal country.

WHY IS IT NAMED *HOT SPOT*?

The town is named for the Hot Spot Coal Company.

WHAT DO YOU NEED TO KNOW ABOUT HOT SPOT?

Chances are, you won't find a whole lot of Internet hot spots in town.

HOWLONG,
AUSTRALIA

Indeed, Howlong? Six inches? Eight inches? Ron Jeremy size? Or, more likely, are we talking microscopic? If so, we've got a simple piece of advice: Stay away from the Australian state of New South Wales.

Why? Because if you go there you might find yourself in Howlong. And if asked . . . Well, do you really want to answer? You might be better off going to Dontaskmehowlong, if, indeed, such a community actually existed somewhere (as far as we know, it doesn't).

How did Howlong become a place that asks a rather impudent question of its residents and visitors?

The story starts, as so many do, with the acquisition of aboriginal lands. Once upon a time, the land around Howlong was called *Hoolong*, which means "beginning of the plains." The land was, um, "owned" by Isaac Rudd. He retained the name. Over time, *Hoolong* became *Howlong*. How? The question is moot. The answer is lost to history.

Nowadays, this small town of some 2,000 people is considered the metropolis among the other, even smaller, towns in this corner of the middle of freaking nowhere. It *is* big enough to have its own Australian-rules football team, and it was "immortalized" by Spiderbait, an Australian band that a handful of people in important countries have heard of. The group recorded a song called "By the Time I Get to Howlong." ↗

WHERE IS HOWLONG?

Howlong is in New South Wales but nowhere near Sydney . . . or anything else for that matter.

WHY IS IT NAMED HOWLONG?

The word derives from an aboriginal term that means "beginning of the plains."

WHAT DO YOU NEED TO KNOW ABOUT HOWLONG?

What the hell is Australian-rules football?

HUMPTULIPS,
WASHINGTON

If you're like most of us, then you probably stay horny most of the time. You're way past getting aroused by Victoria's Secret catalogues. You start to stiffen when you walk past a display of granny panties. But even you have to draw the line *somewhere*. Um, right?

But some folks are even more desperate than you are. Need proof? Well, *someone* had to name Humptulips, Washington, after a flora-flaunting fetish. Hump tulips? Uh, no thanks, dude. I'm fine just humping myself, if necessary.

In truth, there are at least three possible origins for the odd and maybe-too-kinky name of this town in Gray Harbors County. One possibility is that *humptulips* is an indigenous tribe's word for "hard to pole" (snicker) . . . as in, "it's hard to pole our canoes through this river."

Perhaps *humptulips* means "chilly region." Or, finally, the town could be named for a band of the Chehalis tribe.

However Humptulips came to be, the name is pretty damn weird. So weird, in fact, that oddball author Tom Robbins included it in his book, *Another Roadside Attraction.* ↗

PLANT SOME HUMPTULIPS.

Humptulips is a town of roughly two hundred people, in the coastal Washington county of Grays Harbor.

PRUNE YOUR HUMPTULIPS.

Stories vary about how Humptulips got its name, but all of them have to do with a word that originated with indigenous tribes.

TIPTOE THROUGH THE HUMPTULIPS.

Don't go there expecting weird, kinky, freaky sex with a floral species, you fucking weirdo.

HUMPTY DOO,
AUSTRALIA

The Big Boxing Crocodile is pissed. Why? Because people make fun of his hometown. Some call it *humpty dumpty*. Others, remembering the days of old-school hip hop, call it *humpty dance*, after the Digital Undergound's smash. It's enough to make even a giant fiberglass (or whatever he is) figure go apeshit.

Humpty Doo is a small town in Australia's Northern Territory, not far from a city named after Charles Darwin. The current name is a slight change from the name of a station, Umpity Doo, around which the town grew.

Home nowadays to mangos, a giant statue of a boxing crocodile, and not a whole hell of a lot else, the origins of Humpty Doo's name are shrouded in mystery. A few ideas have been suggested, however.

One suggestion is that the town was named for the word *umpty*, an army slang term used in Morse code for the dash symbol. Perhaps the name comes from a slang term that basically means "doing things in a fucked-up way." Most likely, the name is an Anglicization of an aboriginal term meaning "popular resting place."

The name was first used during a hare-brained attempt to grow rice in present-day Humpty Doo. Birds carried off the rice, and the soil in Australia is too salty for rice anyway. Mangos were tried instead, and they have been more successful.

And why, you might ask, is the town lorded over by a giant boxing crocodile? Who the hell knows? ⬈

WHERE IS HUMPTY DOO?

It's near Darwin, in Australia's Northern Territory.

WHY DOES IT HAVE SUCH AN ODD NAME?

Some believe it's due to those rascally aborigines, while others think the name has something to do with military code.

WHAT DO YOU NEED TO KNOW ABOUT HUMPTY DOO?

It is watched over by a giant boxing crocodile.

HUNGRY MOTHER STATE PARK,
VIRGINIA

What kind of name is Hungry Mother State Park? Was it named by hippie freaks who were stoned out of their gourds and having a major attack of the munchies? At least they had the propriety to abridge "Hungry as a Motherfucker" to "Hungry Mother."

Sure, the park itself may be delightful. It offers overnight camping, cabin and boat rentals, and even a conference center. But how the hell can you get any rest with all these hungry mothers around? Damn. Go buy some Cheetos and chill the "f" out.

Actually (violins here), the park's odd name derives from a sad incident designed to make non-Native Americans feel less guilty about the destruction of actual Native Americans.

It seems that some bad injuns were destroying settlements along the New River, which is just south of the state park. A woman named Molly Muller and her child managed to escape from the Indians. They wandered through the wilderness, subsisting on wild berries. Eventually, Molly collapsed. Her child managed to find help and could only whisper the words "hungry mother" when rescued. The child took a search party to Molly, who had died. Yes, it's a sad story.

But how do we know if it's true? Who's to say that, in fact, the park wasn't named by rabid fans of Frank Zappa and the Mothers of Invention? Hmm? It just doesn't sound as romantic, that's all. ⤴

WHERE IS HUNGRY MOTHER STATE PARK?

It's in the southwestern part of Virginia, just off Interstate 81.

WHY IS IT NAMED HUNGRY MOTHER?

The name is related to an attack by wild-eyed injuns.

WHAT DO YOU NEED TO KNOW ABOUT HUNGRY MOTHER STATE PARK?

Attempts to change the name to Hungry Motherfucker State Park have, thus far, failed.

I.X.L.,
OKLAHOMA

OMG! WTF! LMFAO! WTH is I.X.L.? And who ever thought that it would make a ripping good name for a town? Some folks in Oklahoma, that's who. From the state that brought you Loco (see page 123) comes, possibly, the oddest name in this book, apart from Zzyzx, California (see page 201).

First of all, how many towns have initials for names? Um . . . can't think of any. And if you *are* going to ascribe initials to your town, then shouldn't they be something meaningful like FDR, JFK, or MLK? Secondly, agreement about just what the fuck *I.X.L.* stands for does not exist.

Some conjecture that the letters are really Roman numerals, but no one seems to know the significance of these numbers. Others suggest the name means "I excel," as in, "I'm really good at this." But *that* makes little sense because at what do the folks in this Podunk town excel? Cow tipping? Shit-kicking?

According to a story from a local news channel, I.X.L. most likely owes its name to Native Americans. The name is made up of a hodgepodge of letters from the names of the man who bought the land and the Indian who sold the land.

None of these theories really sound all that great. It's still a pretty freaking bizarre name for a town in the middle of Oklahoma. Just do like most people . . . stay the hell out of this godforsaken state. ➐

WHERE IS I.X.L.?
It's in Oklahoma's Okfuskee (!!) County, right about in the middle of the state.

WHY IS IT NAMED I.X.L.?
Answers vary. Perhaps a better question is: Who the fuck cares?

WHAT DO YOU NEED TO KNOW ABOUT I.X.L.?
Absolutely nothing.

IDIOT CREEK,
OREGON

How would you like to live along the banks of a gentle creek, which ripples through a pristine, snowy landscape? Does this sound like paradise? Then you're an Idiot . . . Creek, that is.

Idiot Creek owes its name to the town of Idiotville (seriously). Now a ghost town, Idiotville once was a remote logging community. Folks claimed the place was so hard to get to that only an idiot would work there. Over time, the idiots who worked there became proud of being self-proclaimed idiots, so the community became known as Idiotville.

Eventually, folks realized they actually *were* idiots to live in the middle of freaking nowhere, so the town died. Before it breathed its last municipal breath, the loggers in the community named a nearby creek after the town, and Idiot Creek it remains.

Most likely, this body of water is now a place where teenagers dare each other to do really stupid things. There they go, in little gangs like lemmings, to get really wasted and do back flips into the creek from three stories up.

Yep. It's these young people in Tillamook County who proudly keep the state's idiot banner flying. ➚

WHERE IS IDIOT CREEK?

It's in Tillamook County, Oregon, along the banks of Idiotville.

WHY IS IT SUCH AN IDIOT?

At one time, it was said that you'd have to be an idiot to work in a particularly remote logging community. Thus, Idiotville was born, and from it, Idiot Creek.

WHAT DO YOU NEED TO KNOW ABOUT IDIOT CREEK?

The town of Idiotville is now abandoned, but the creek keeps on flowing idiotically.

INACCESSIBLE ISLAND,
UNITED KINGDOM TERRITORY

In some parts of the United States there's a saying: You can't get there from here. It's a straightforward statement along the lines of, "Dude, you're so lost you're totally fucked," that people from outside the region take for some nugget of philosophical wisdom.

There are some places on Earth that truly are inaccessible: the tops of very tall mountains, the depths of the ocean, Antarctica. One was considered so out of the way that, to this day, it is called Inaccessible Island. The island in the South Atlantic Ocean first was spotted by Portuguese sailors who made note of it but did not explore it. Good call. The island contained no booty . . . of the treasure or the female variety. About 150 years later, Dutch sailors landed on the island and called it *Inaccessible* because all they could explore was the beach due to many rocky cliffs. If they'd made it over the cliffs, they would have found . . . a bunch of penguins. Wow!

Since Inaccessible is some 2,000 miles from South Africa, the nearest mainland, it also remains pretty much inaccessible except to extremely hardy scientists. Due to its remoteness and lack of humans, Inaccessible Island is a protected wildlife reserve.

If you ever find yourself on Inaccessible Island because, say, your folks get tired of having you live in their basement so they banish you to the archipelago, then you will have plenty of solitude. And, since your love life has been nonexistent, you may find a happy and willing penguin partner. Happy hunting! ↗

WHERE IS THIS INCONVENIENT PLACE?

Inaccessible Island is in the middle of the South Atlantic Ocean, thousands of miles from any mainland.

WHY IS IT NAMED *INACCESSIBLE ISLAND*?

Early explorers found the interior of the island "inaccessible" due to rocky cliffs.

WHAT DO YOU NEED TO KNOW ABOUT INACCESSIBLE ISLAND?

It's a protected wildlife reserve.

KAKA,
ARIZONA

Kaka happens. In fact, it happens all over the world. There's Kaka in Turkmenistan. There's Kaka in New Zealand. There's Kaka in the Congo. But you don't have to travel halfway around the world to find a community with a name that's a euphemism for "shit."

Some fifty miles south of Phoenix, Arizona, is the tiny town of Kaka. Folks in the community work in Kaka businesses, drive Kaka cars, make love to their Kaka wives and husbands. There's just Kaka everywhere!

How, you might ask, did this community get its shitty name? Blame the Tohono O'odham, a tribe associated with the southwestern United States. The tribe was formerly known as the *Papago*, but contemporary tribal members have rejected the name because it was a derogatory one given to them by Spanish conquistadors. But enough about history . . . back to Kaka!

In the Tohono O'odham language, *kaka* means "clearing." Apparently, the tiny town of Kaka is in a clearing. The name makes perfect sense, then, doesn't it? Except that . . . it sounds like shit. Why did the people of this community choose to pay homage to aboriginal Americans by adopting the name *Kaka*?

Didn't the tribe have *any* other words that could have been deemed acceptable for a fledgling town's name? *Kaka*? Um, Earth to Kaka . . . your town name sounds like shit! Please. Leave the Kaka in Africa and Turkmenistan, wherever the fuck *that* is. ↗

WHERE IS KAKA?

In your pants after a shart.

WHY IS IT NAMED AFTER SHIT?

Actually, *Kaka* is a Tohono O'odham word for "clearing."

WHAT DO YOU NEED TO KNOW ABOUT KAKA?

Folks in town thought it would be a good idea to name their community after a euphemism for shit.

KILL,
IRELAND

Man, you've got to be one angry, vengeful mother-fucker to want to kill Ireland. That's a country of 6.3 million people! Who would make Guinness? What band would music magazines compare to Jesus if U2 were wiped off the planet? And are leprechauns included in that population figure?

The mind reels. Yet, there is one insurgent community within Ireland that, apparently, has its sites set on mass destruction. The method will have to be guerilla warfare because Kill, in the County Kildare, only has a population of 2,500.

The folks in Kill are clever. They claim that the town's name is derived from the Gaelic word, *chill*, which means church. And the town does, in fact, have at least two churches within its borders.

But we know better about these bloodthirsty ass-holes. Kill has been a regular winner of the National Tidy Towns competition, and it's no wonder. Anyone who dares to leave a scrap of paper on their front yard or to be in any way untidy is probably rounded up and summarily shot.

Kill may be a nice, bucolic village, but watch out. These fuckers mean business. ↗

WHERE IS KILL?
This town of 2,500 is in the County Kildare.

WHY DOES IT HAVE SUCH A VIOLENT NAME?
The town's name probably derives from a Gaelic word that means "church," but you never know, these guys could turn violent at any time.

WHAT DO YOU NEED TO KNOW ABOUT KILL?
It's apparently very tidy.

KINKI,
JAPAN

It is quite surprising that in the button-down country of Japan, which presents a face of solidity and conformity to the rest of the world, there is a town that would proclaim proudly its kinkiness. Yet, that's exactly what has been done not just in one community but in one entire region!

It's true! The Kinki region lies in Japan's south-central region. Sure, some locals will call it the Kansai region, but don't be fooled! They're probably just afraid to admit how Kinki they truly are.

This particular part of Japan has been Kinki for nearly 2,000 years. During the sixth century, Japan established several provinces near its capital. Collectively, these provinces became Kinki. Both *Kinki* and *Kansai* supposedly mean something along the lines of, "area around or near the capital," but we are certain that the TRUE translation is "island of the kinky freaks who dig bondage porn and superb hookers." ⬈

WHERE IS KINKI?

Japan's Kinki region is in the country's south-central region.

WHY IS IT CALLED *KINKI*?

The Japanese *claim* that *Kinki* means "the neighborhood of the capital" or something to that effect.

WHAT DO YOU NEED TO KNOW ABOUT KINKI?

Go now! The region is filled with more than 20 million Kinki people!

KNOB LICK,
MISSOURI

The view from Knob Lick Mountain is breathtaking. In the foreground, you see pristine farmland and houses that could have come straight from Norman Rockwell paintings. Off in the distance stand the gently sloping Ozark Mountains.

It's a truly beautiful part of America. There's only one real problem. Live there, and you live in a place named for a euphemism for oral sex. You know, giving head? Getting some brain? And, most appropriately, slobbering on the knob?

Like other places in this book that contain *knob* or *lick* in their names, there's a perfectly good explanation as to why this small Missouri community is named "Knob Lick." It's the head-giving capital of the nation, that's why.

In fact, around these (hillbilly-laden) parts, a *knob* is the name given to an isolated mountain with a bare summit. And a *lick* is a place of natural salt deposits that animals lick for their nutritive qualities. Hence, Knob Lick.

But does it really matter how reasonable an explanation exists for the name of this community and its nearby mountain? Admit it. You wouldn't be caught dead in a community named for blow jobs. And you're not alone. The unincorporated community has a pretty sparse population. ➚

HAVE YOU SEEN KNOB LICK?

Sure. It's near the agricultural community of Farmington, Missouri. You know where that is, right?

WHY IS THIS COMMUNITY NAMED FOR ORAL SEX?

Well, it isn't really. A *knob* in them-thar parts is an isolated mountain without any vegetation on its summit. And a *lick* is what you get in the backseat of your AMC Gremlin, if you're lucky. Oh, and it's also what folks around those parts call a place with natural salt deposits that animals lick.

WHAT DO YOU NEED TO KNOW ABOUT KNOB LICK?

It's a very pretty community, a very pretty community that appears to be named for blow jobs.

KNOCKEMSTIFF,
OHIO

First off . . . did anyone else know there are ghost towns in Ohio? Aren't all the ghost towns like, out west or something? Apparently not. One of them is in Ohio, and maybe there's nobody left because they all got bitch slapped into the great oblivion. What else can you expect from a place called Knockemstiff?

Stories abound to explain the name of this frontier town. One suggests that, when the community first was born, a massive donnybrook broke out. Or, would you believe that the name was a minister's advice to a woman complaining about her husband's cheating ways? Or, then again, maybe the name is slang for moonshine.

The latter is the most likely, since this particular part of Ohio was once a haven of moonshiners, all roaring down thunder road with their trunks full of greased lightning. Well, when the town was born, there weren't any cars. But there were certainly many stills.

Nowadays, the ghost town has a reputation for just that: ghosts. Spirits of the not-knock-you-on-your-ass variety are said to include a permanently foggy dip in the road—in which a ghostly smoking man sometimes resides along with the ghost of a person who committed suicide by leaping from cliffs in the area. Apparently, you can hear him scream all the way from the cliff to the ground.

The hell with that. Just keep pouring that moonshine. ↗

WHERE IS KNOCKEMSTIFF?

Knockemstiff is in Ross County, near Chillicothe.

WHY KNOCKEMSTIFF?

The name may be related to brawling, a cheating husband, or to moonshine. Who cares about Knockemstiff?

GHOSTS SEEM TO LIKE THIS GHOST TOWN.

Many eerie stories abound in the area. Or maybe everybody's just so blitzed on illicit booze that they're seeing things. Who knows? Who cares?

LAKE CHARGOGGAGOGGMAN-CHAUGGAGOGGCHAUBUNAGUN-GAMAUGG,
MASSACHUSETTS

You'd think people would be happy enough with the name Lake Chaubunagungamaug, right? I mean, if you're hoping to win the "longest name in America" contest, then you'd think Lake Chaubunagungamaug is sufficient. Look at that freaking word. It's seventeen letters long. But noooooooooooooo. The friendly folks in Webster, Massachusetts don't want you to shorten their lake's name from what they consider its real name: Lake Chargoggagoggmanchauggagogg-gchaubunagungamaugg. Webster citizens cling to this longer version of the lake's name and feel pleased with themselves that they can prounounce it.

Lake Chargoggagoggmanchauggagoggchaubuna-gungamaugg gets its name from the indigenous Nipmuc people. It translates roughly to "neutral fishing area" since the lake was used by many tribes, not all of which got along.

In recent years, many folks in the area have just started calling the body of water Lake Webster. This name makes older residents apoplectic because, well, because they're old and don't have anything better to do than to bitch about young whippersnappers shortening the name of their lake from forty-five to seven letters. Get a life! Oh, wait. You're old. Dang, die already! ↗

▶ WHERE IS THIS UNPRONOUNCE-ABLE LAKE?

Lake Chargoggag-oggmanchauggagog-gchaubunagungam-augg is in Webster, Massachusetts. Piss someone off up there by calling the body of water *Lake Webster*.

▶ WTF IS UP WITH THE NAME?

It's Nipmuc for, basically, "Neutral Lake." The Nipmucs, who can't even spell their own tribe's name— sometimes it contains a "k" after the "s," and sometimes it doesn't—should not be charged with naming anything.

▶ WHAT DO I NEED TO KNOW ABOUT LAKE CHARGOGGAGOGG-MANCHAUGGAGOGG-GCHAUBUNAGUN-GAMAUGG?

It's got a long god-dam name.

LAKE TITICACA,
PERU AND BOLIVIA

Breasts and thongs? Good. Breasts and beer? Good. Breasts and turds? Um . . . not so good. But don't let that stop you from contemplating one of the most beautiful spots in the world: Lake Titicaca.

The name is a clusterfuck of indigenous words, which could mean anything from "puma head," because the lake supposedly looks like that from above, to "hunting grounds" or "Walmart sucks."

Ask an Inca, those cool guys from the area who partied hardy every year during the annual Festival of the Sun passing around corn beer and watching a high priest remove the pulsating and quivering organs from a pure black or white llama, followed no doubt by some orgies. Party!

Lake Titicaca forms part of the border between the South American countries Peru and Bolivia, two emerging drug strongholds, and—at more than two miles above sea level—Lake Titicaca is the perfect place to get high. Don't bogart that peyote, my friend. ↗

JUST WHERE IS THIS CA-CA?

Lake Titicaca forms a portion of the border between Peru and Bolivia. There's no official word on who claims the titty portion of the lake and who claims the ca-ca portion of the lake.

WHY IS IT NAMED FOR TITTIES?

Titicaca is, most likely, a mishmash of words from the languages of local indigenous people. Or it was named by ancient Incan fifth graders.

HOW TO KNOW SHIT ABOUT CA-CA . . .

At 12,500 feet above sea level, Lake Titicaca is higher than your wastoid college roommate. At 3,200 square miles, Lake Titicaca is the largest lake in South America . . . bigger than any "moose" you ever scammed on while wearing beer goggles.

LAYMAN,
OHIO

You are comfortable with your masculinity. You have no problem being assertive or aggressive, and you're proud to tell people that you hail from Layman. When people make homophobic jokes, you're fine. Maybe you're crying on the inside, but you're laughing on the outside.

Layman, Ohio, was named for Amos Layman, a Democrat, who established the, um, *Marietta Republican* in 1849. He may not have been the brightest bulb in the greenhouse (Dude, you're a *Democrat*, not a *Republican*), but he was still deemed worthy of naming a town after.

One wonders if Mr. Layman was comfortable with his feminine side. Surely his detractors were just as immature as those who cast stones today. No doubt, they suggested he liked to "lay" the occasional "man" . . . not that there's anything wrong with that. Right? ↗

SPENDING TIME INSIDE LAYMAN

Layman is in Ohio's Washington County, in the state's Parkersburg-Marietta metropolitan area.

ENJOYING LAYMAN.

Layman was named for a Democrat, Amos Layman, who started a newspaper named the *Marietta Republican*. Perhaps he was an idiot?

CAN YOU TAKE ME TO LAYMAN?

Layman is just the spot for you, macho man. You can stay at the local YMCA.

LICKING COUNTY,
OHIO

By now, you've probably learned that some spots in the world contain salt licks. These are like candy stores to roaming animals and have been since the world was still populated by mammoths and saber-tooth tigers. One particular spot in Ohio is so rife with salt licks that it has been named Licking County.

Yes, we know what you're thinking. It's not unusual for communities to name themselves after geographical landmarks. Pilot Mountain, North Carolina, is near Pilot Mountain, for example. Okeechobee, Florida, is named for Lake Okeechobee. But, Ohio, *news flash . . . Licking County* was a poor choice for a name.

Do you really want tourists to come to town and take Licking photos? Do you want to buy stuff at Licking grocery stores? And don't even get us started on the concept of Licking gas. Gross.

You could have named the place *Salt Lick County.* That's not particularly funny or disturbing, and it still pays homage to your area's resources. But, no. In your past, some genius or geniuses decided to opt for *Licking County.* Now you guys sound like a bunch of kinky beasts, out to lick anything that moves (or that *doesn't* move, for that matter). ↗

WHERE IS LICKING COUNTY, OHIO?

It's just about smack dab in the middle of the state, not too far from Columbus.

WHY IS IT NAMED *LICKING COUNTY*?

Because the people there like to lick things. A lot. Including things they probably shouldn't be licking. Or, maybe, the county is named for its predominance of salt licks.

WHAT DO YOU NEED TO KNOW ABOUT LICKING COUNTY?

It's a great place to take Licking photos.

LIZARD LICK,
NORTH CAROLINA

God bless the South and all its toothless, brainless, drunken reprobates! Where else would we get towns with such freaking great names as Toad Suck (see page 175) and Lizard Lick. No, these places weren't named because they are bastions of bestiality—though they might well be. Instead, they owe their names to heavy drinking.

In the late 1800s, the federal government built a still near the present site of Lizard Lick. The feds were tired of losing money to illegal moonshine. Now it seems the still attracted lizards to the fence around the property because the still itself attracted all kinds of insects. Sugar is used in fermentation. Remember, dumb ass?

Supposedly, the official whiskey taster (God-DAMN what a great job that would be!) was a gent named Ed Pulley, who sported a walking cane. After a hard day's work, he would knock the lizards off the fence with his cane, which he took to calling the "lizard licker."

If this story sounds like total bullshit . . . you're wrong again. To this day, Lizard Lick remains, even though the stills are gone. Drunken students from nearby North Carolina State University must content themselves with drinking cheap liquor at frat parties. ⤴

WHERE CAN YOU LICK LIZARDS?

Jesus, are you a sick motherfucker, or what? If you're talking about the town of Lizard Lick, it's in North Carolina's Wake County.

WHY IS IT CALLED LIZARD LICK?

Long story short... alcohol, lizards, a drunken guy with a cane.

WHAT DO YOU NEED TO KNOW ABOUT LIZARD LICK?

It does a brisk bumper sticker and souvenir license plate business.

THE LIZZIE BORDEN BED AND BREAKFAST,
FALL RIVER, MASSACHUSETTS

Clearly, time heals all wounds. Think about it this way. If it were still around, would you *really* want to vacation in former serial killer Jeffrey Dahmer's apartment? Or, say, a former home of the BTK Killer? Most people would opt for other locales for romantic weekend getaways. That said, scores of people have no qualms whatsoever visiting Fall River and getting reacquainted in a home that inspired one of the "Trials of the Century." What makes it acceptable, apparently, is that the century in question is the nineteenth.

In 1892, Lizzie Borden allegedly took an ax and gave her step-mother forty whacks. In fact, it was more like twenty. But forty makes for a much cooler jump-rope rhyme. Afterward, Lizzie killed her father. The crime was sensational, back in those simpler times when everyone was kind to others, unless those others were, say, gay or black or Chinese or something.

Just like O.J., Lizzie was acquitted of the murder. And just like O.J., no one else was ever tried for the murder. But as far as the public was concerned, Lizzie was a vicious psychopath.

Now, you can relive the elder Bordens' horrifying last moments. You can stay in the room where Mrs. Borden lay chopped into kindling or sit on the very couch on which Mr. Borden's body was found. And if you like that, we'd like to sell you Ted Bundy's toothbrush. Cheap. Any takers? ↗

WHERE IS LIZZIE'S PLACE?

The B & B is in the Fall River, Massachusetts, house where the murders took place over one hundred years ago.

WHY IS IT CALLED THE LIZZIE BORDEN BED & BREAKFAST?

I just answered that. Aren't you paying attention?

WHAT DO YOU NEED TO KNOW ABOUT LIZZIE'S PLACE?

You can stay in the room where Lizzie's step-mother was killed, if you're into that sort of thing, you sick motherfucker.

LLANFAIRPWLLGWYNGYLLGO-GERYCHWYRNDROBWLLLLAN-TYSILIOGOGOGOCH,

WALES

At first, it seems mildly impressive that this small Welsh town has the longest name in the United Kingdom. Sure, no one can pronounce it—probably not even Llanfairpwllgwyngyllgogerychwyrndrob-wllllantysiliogogogochites—but that's not *their* fault, right? They just got saddled with a bitch of a name, and, well shit, why *not* use that name to attract the odd tourist or two. Wrong! It turns out that the name is a modern invention. Well . . . sort of modern. It's not ancient anyway. The name was contrived in the 1860s in an effort to give the town's train station the longest place name in the UK. Yep, that's right. The name is a publicity stunt, akin to Truth or Consequences, New Mexico (see page 179) or DISH, Texas (see page 64).

The Welsh translation of the name is "St. Mary's Church in the hollow of the white hazel near to the rapid whirlpool of Llantysilio of the red cave." Now, the town's original name, "Llanfair Pwllgwyngyll," was lengthy and almost impossible to pronounce, but the town, in an early example of creative marketing, adopted the even longer and even more impossible to pronounce, Llanfairpwllgwyngyllgogerychwyrndrob-wllllantysiliogogogoch.

Strangely, folks have not been flocking to the town for the last 140 years. ↗

WHERE IS LLANFAIRPWLL-GWYNGYLLGO-GERYCHWYRN-DROBWLLLLANTYSI-LIOGOGOGOCH?

It's in Wales, on the island of Angelsey.

WHY IS IT NAMED *LLANFAIRPWLLG-WYNGYLLGOGERY-CHWYRNDROB-WLLLLANTYSIL-IOGOGOGOCH*?

It was developed as a publicity stunt, basically.

WHAT DO YOU NEED TO KNOW ABOUT LLANFAIR-PWLLGWYNGYLL-GOGERYCHWYRN-DROBWLLLLANTYSI-LIOGOGOGOCH?

Other towns in the United Kingdom have considered even longer names, as though it were a genuine honor to have the longest place name in the UK.

LOCO,
OKLAHOMA

Some might say you'd be "loco" to live in Oklahoma. Period. Sure, it's home to Oral Roberts University and its super cool "prayer tower" as well as to a school with a pretty good football team, but, overall, there's not much to the place. Nonetheless, we found it difficult to believe that a town within the state actually admits to being Loco.

Maybe they can blame their insanity on Texas, which has helped launch the career of many particularly crazy politicians from both parties. Loco is in a county just north of the Texas border.

But, no! The town blames its insanity on locoweed. For the uninitiated, *locoweed* is rarely used slang for marijuana. It *also* refers to any of a number of plants that cause intoxication in livestock that choose it for grazing. Sure, it's cool to think of drunk cattle, but the animals usually eat so much of the stuff that they wind up with cell damage or heart failure. PETA, take note!

Loco, Oklahoma, may simply have liked the assonance caused by putting these names together, but they chose *Loco* because of incidents involving locoweed and livestock. So, basically, unlike Weed (see page 189), this Oklahoma town actually *is* named for an intoxicating substance. Sweet, bro. Maybe Oklahoma isn't so awful after all. ↗

> **WHERE IS LOCO?**
> Loco is in Oklahoma's Stephens County, just north of the Texas border.

> **WHY IS IT NAMED LOCO?**
> Loco is named for the presence of locoweed, plants that intoxicate livestock, in the area.

> **WHAT DO YOU NEED TO KNOW ABOUT LOCO?**
> No, you should NOT try to get a legal high from eating or smoking plants made from locoweed.

LOONEYVILLE,
TEXAS

Thanks to the two-term presidency of transplanted Texan George W. Bush, most people consider Texas pretty batty. Sure, Crawford, Texas, is ground zero for stupidity and nuttiness, but if you can't make it there, then you could always visit Looneyville.

Looneyville takes its name from a businessman, John Looney, who helped develop the community by opening numerous ventures just after the Civil War. Over time, Looneyville has dwindled away to very few residents. Perhaps they just don't like describing themselves as Looneys.

Fortunately, even though most human residents have left the town, Looneyville has become a retirement community for anthropomorphic bunnies, ducks, pigs, cats, and tweety birds, thus ensuring that the community will thrive in perpetuity. ⤴

WHERE IS LOONEYVILLE?

Looneyville is near Nacogdoches, Texas, and not far from the Louisiana border.

WHY IS IT NAMED *LOONEYVILLE*?

It was named for forty-third president, George W. Bush. Or, maybe it was named for a businessman who settled the area in the 1870s.

WHAT DO YOU NEED TO KNOW ABOUT LOONEYVILLE?

It's Dick Cheney's hometown.

LOST,
SCOTLAND

Ah, shit. We're lost. Will you go and ask someone where we are? Dang. Why did we decide to hitch around the wilds of Scotland? We're never going to find Aberdeen now. So, dude, where are we? What? Say that again? Well, no shit, genius. I know we're lost.

Stop being an asshole and tell me where we are, so I can find it on the map. What? Dude. If you don't stop saying we're lost, I'm going to kick your ass. Wait. What did you say? That's the name of this freaking place? Are you shitting me?

No, it's true. Lost is a real place in Scotland. In Scottish Gaelic, the community's name is *Losda*, which comes from the Gaelic word *taigh osda*, which means "inn." Anglicization of the name has resulted in a town that is permanently Lost. The irony is that, due to a popular television show, folks are finding Lost in order to steal its town signs. Thefts became so rampant that the town's leaders tried to change the community's name to Lost Farm . . . to no avail.

Locals like being Lost. They'd been Lost for hundreds of years. Why, all of the sudden, should they be found *now*? So, Lost continues to be a town in Scotland. And Lost's signs continue to fill up the dorm rooms of bratty, drunken college kids the world over. ↗

WHERE CAN YOU FIND LOST?

Lost is forty miles from Aberdeen.

WHY IS IT LOST?

Lost is derived from a Scottish Gaelic word meaning "inn."

WHAT DO YOU NEED TO KNOW ABOUT LOST?

If the folks there were smart, they would have sued the shit out of the producers of the TV show of the same name.

LOVELADIES,
NEW JERSEY

Now, *here's* a town for all the playas. It's an oasis of the Garden State, where one can "tap dat" and "hit dat" (i.e., have meaningless sex) to one's heart's content. That's right. If you love the ladies, then run—don't walk—to Loveladies, New Jersey.

Oh, wait a minute. The name is just an accident. Nope, what you're a hell of a lot more likely to find in Loveladies is bored rich people with formaldehyde in their veins. On second thought . . . the community probably has a myriad of bored MILF's just dying for some young studs. Loveladies might, in fact, be a great place to visit.

The name *Loveladies* is related to the community's past as a lifeguard station. A small island just off the coast of the station was owned by a man named Thomas Lovelady. Over time, the entire area came to be called Lovelady's and, finally, Loveladies.

The community, part of the Longbeach Township, has become a McMansion-lover's paradise . . . giant homes fill up most available land. Rich folks, who rarely take advantage of their homes' lovely views, sit inside while illegal immigrants fix up their lawns and serve as cabana boys.

Fortunately, for all you MILF hunters, Loveladies is filled with public beaches. So, grab some sunblock, a pocket full of condoms, and head for this small New Jersey community. When they're not locked in cabana boy embraces, the desperate housewives of Loveladies may come out for some new fun in the sun. ↗

WHERE IS LOVELADIES?

Loveladies is a very tiny community along the Jersey Shore; it's part of the Long-beach Township.

WHY IS IT NAMED LOVELADIES?

A man named Thomas Lovelady once owned a small island off the coast of the community. Over time, "Lovelady's" became "Loveladies."

WHAT DO YOU NEED TO KNOW ABOUT LOVELADIES?

It's filled with MILFs, so go visit. What have you got to lose?

LOWER BALL'S FALLS,
CANADA

Yes, there's also an Upper Ball's Falls, but, somehow, *Lower Ball's Falls* just sounds funnier. One pictures an old guy whose testicles have descended to an alarming degree, sitting on an orthopedic sofa, cradling his massive family jewels in specially made jockeys . . . or something equally bizarre and disgusting.

George Ball built several mills along Twenty Mile Creek in Ontario. How did he get the land? By selling out Americans during the Revolutionary War. For his efforts, the Crown gave him the huge parcel of land. Asshole. Anyway . . . he built these mills, and a town grew up around them. The town's name? *Ball's Falls*, of course!

Over time, Ball's empire dwindled away, and his hamlet became a ghost town, a gentle reminder of falling balls. However, people clamored to see these falls of Ball's, and the site later was restored to its turn-of-the-nineteenth-century glory by the Niagara Peninsula Conservations Authority.

So, now *you* can enjoy seeing Lower Ball's Falls. Take in the majestic views and old-timey buildings left over from a quieter time. And even if your own balls are falling, be thankful that you chose to vacation *here*, rather than in Pennsylvania's Blue Ball (see page 24). ↗

WHERE IS LOWER BALL'S FALLS?

Upper and Lower Ball's Falls are located on the site of a now-abandoned company town— called Ball's Falls—in Ontario, not far from Niagara Falls.

WHY IS IT CALLED LOWER BALL'S FALLS?

To distinguish it from Upper Ball's Falls, obviously. Dumb ass.

WHAT DO YOU NEED TO KNOW ABOUT LOWER BALL'S FALLS?

It sounds painful.

MAIDENHEAD,
ENGLAND

It's okay to admit that you haven't had sex in a long time . . . probably ever, right? Sure, you should feel embarrassed about this fact, but you don't have to, like, kill yourself over it or anything. In fact, we're here to help you!

Some twenty-five miles from London is a city that, if its name is any indication, is just filled to bursting with horny virgins. You see, *maidenhead* is a quaint term for a woman's virginity, as in, "She still possessed her maidenhead on her wedding night."

Shakespeare's heroines are always concerned about their maidenheads, and his male characters often make puns about women's virginity that include references to maidenheads. Since you've never opened a volume of Shakespeare in your life, we just thought we'd inform you of this maidenhead fact.

Moving on . . . the town of Maidenhead, bountiful virgins and all, gets its name from its riverside area where the so-called *new wharf*, or *maiden hythe*, was built during Anglo-Saxon times. Only in England could something *new* be over a thousand years old.

There's more good news for you. Not only is Maidenhead filled with hungry virgins, but it's also England's Silicon Valley. So, all the women must get promised, at birth, free silicon implants. Oh, wait . . . that's silicone, with an "e." All they produce in Maidenhead is computer chips. Bummer. ↗

WHERE IS MAIDENHEAD?

You won't find it among any of the women *you've* been talking to lately.

WHY IS IT CALLED MAIDENHEAD?

The name comes from Saxon words, *maiden hythe*, which mean "new wharf."

WHAT DO YOU NEED TO KNOW ABOUT MAIDENHEAD?

It is considered England's Silicon Valley.

MEAT CAMP,
NORTH CAROLINA

Hey, baby, I got your Meat Camp . . . swingin'! This is the sign that welcomes visitors to a small and oddly named town in North Carolina's Watauga County. Just kidding. It's too damn small (kind of like your meat) to have a sign. Nonetheless, people travel from miles around to check out all the meat on display.

Actually, Meat Camp is on land once owned by Daniel Boone—yes, *that* Daniel Boone. The actual "meat camp" was a cabin in which hunters stored their meat and pelts as they went to shoot at more animals. Dang . . . why hasn't PETA put some sort of smack down on this community? Or lodged some effort to rename the place Tofu Camp or Soy Camp or something?

The 3,000 or so residents of Meat Camp are proud. The men of Meat Camp are hardy sorts, pleased with their meat. The ladies, of course, are all very happy as well. They get their meat on demand, and it's always satisfying.

They worship on Sundays at Meat Camp Church or at Meat Camp Baptist Church (no, really), where they learn to worship at the altar of Col. Sanders, Señor Taco Bell, and Ronald McDonald, all well-known purveyors of fine, fine meat. Yes, life's good in lil ol' Meat Camp. ↗

I'VE GOT YOUR MEAT CAMP RIGHT HERE.

Meat Camp is in North Carolina's Watauga County, nestled in the mountains near Boone.

GET OFF MY MEAT CAMP.

Meat Camp, on land once owned by Daniel Boone, was home to a cabin in which hunters and traders stored meat and pelts while they went back to kill more animals.

COME ON, BABY . . . WORK MY MEAT CAMP.

PETA, are you asleep at the switch? Meat is murder! Let's make this place Tofu Camp right away!

MEXICAN HAT,
UTAH

You expect to find Mexicans in Arizona, New Mexico, Texas, and so on. In fact, you expect to find them throughout the United States. But one place you might not associate with our neighbors from south of the border is Utah.

Utah conjures up images of white people—*extremely* white people—who possess perfect teeth, perhaps some dimples, and a belief in a religion that has to do with golden plates left in the American Southwest by aliens (from outer space, not illegal ones) . . . or something like that.

Consequently, if you were to learn that a community called *Mexican Hat* exists within the United States, you'd probably expect to find it in, say, Texas or California. But no! You will find the town of Mexican Hat—why not just call it *Sombrero*?—in Utah, of all places.

The tiny community of Mexican Hat can be found in the southeast corner of the state, along the San Juan River. Why is this community which, according to 2000 census figures, has no Mexicans, named *Mexican Hat*, you ask? The town is near a rock formation crowned by rocks that do, in fact, resemble an upside-down sombrero.

So, there you have it. A state that is nearly 50 percent Mormon contains a monument to a country that is mostly Roman Catholic. Now you know. Do you care? ↗

¡OLE! WHERE IS MEXICAN HAT?

Mexican Hat is in Utah's southeast corner, along the San Juan River.

WHY IS IT CALLED *MEXICAN HAT*?

There is a pile of rocks near the town that appears to be topped by an upside-down sombrero.

WHAT DO YOU NEED TO KNOW ABOUT MEXICAN HAT?

The town contains no actual Mexicans.

MIANUS RIVER,
CONNECTICUT

The next time some jerk has the temerity to say you can't find your ass with both hands and a flashlight, just adopt a shit-eating grin and say, "Shows what you know. My anus is in Connecticut."

The Mianus River and the Mianus River Gorge are named for an Indian chief, Myanos, who was killed in 1683. In no time at all, American settlers gave smallpox and a delightful assortment of STDs to Myanos's tribesmen, pretty much wiping them out. Now, as revenge, New Yorkers spend time fishing in, wading in, maybe even drinking from, a river that means the same thing as "asshole."

A buttload of the area around the gorge is a nature preserve, allowing visitors to explore Mianus at their leisure. Who knows what nuggets might be pulled forth from its waters?

Maybe you'll enjoy the area so much you'll invite your buddies to pop a squat on a log or stool and say, "I hope you'll enjoy Mianus as much as I do." ↗

WHERE IS MIANUS?

You mean you don't know? What . . . can't you tell your ass from a hole in the ground? It's in Connecticut, butt munch, and it empties into the Long Island Sound.

HOW THE DEUCE DID MIANUS GET ITS NAME?

Liberal Guilt Alert: Mianus is a variation of Myanos, a Wappinger Confederacy Chief, who died in the region now home to non-Native Americans who could not keep away from Mianus.

WHAT DO YOU NEED TO KNOW ABOUT MIANUS?

Do you really want me to answer that?

MIDDELFART,
DENMARK

If you're not the first fart or the last fart, then what are you? Answer: You're the Middelfart, of course. Man, folks in Denmark must just love it when Americans come to town and make jokes about how their town is named after an embarrassing expulsion of gas.

And quite a bit of gas, at that. You've got to rip off several in order to have a Middelfart, right? Maybe the town is named for "jumping jack farts," the kind of crepitation that takes place when a gas attack hits you during exercise. You can hold those farts in when you're up in the air, but when you land, all bets are off, and you just have to hope that no one else can hear—or smell—your handiwork. If they do, blame your gas on that geek that nobody likes.

Middelfart, in fact, means "central passage." The town was a ferry stop midway between the island of Funen and the peninsula of Jutland. And it also was filled with not-very-bright whale hunters.

For some four hundred years, Middelfartians? Middelfartners? tried to make their community a center of the blubber-mining industry. There was only one problem: The only common whale-like animal in Danish waters is the harbour porpoise. They're not all that big, so their blubber and oil didn't amount to a fart in the wind. And, with the advent of electricity, whale hunting pretty much squeaked out in Middelfart.

Nowadays, it's just a town that appears to be named for flatulence. ↗

WHO (MIDDEL) FARTED?

Middelfart is on the Danish island of Funen and is part of the East Jutland metropolitan area, which has 1.2 million (flatulent) souls.

DID SOMEBODY STEP ON A DUCK?

No. *Middelfart* means "middle passage," or at least that's what the Danes claim.

PULL MY FINGER.

Middelfart tried for centuries to be a whale-hunting capital of the world, but there just aren't any whales there to speak of.

MILK SHAKES,
WASHINGTON

Picture this: You're a lonely prospector or cowboy or logger who hasn't gotten any in a really, really, really long time. Hell, you probably don't have to stretch *your* imagination too far in order to imagine a similar state.

Anyway, you're slogging through the mountains of Columbia County, Washington when you see them: massive, gargantuan, enormous breasts sticking straight up from the Earth like a gift from a God almost as horny as you.

They're not a mirage. They're the twin peaks known as Milk Shakes. The original name given to the peaks by early settlers, *Twin Tits* (no joke), was, apparently, just a little too risqué. So, there you have it: Milk Shakes.

They stick up more than a mile above the surrounding forest, and, to this day, they give lonely, horny, pretty-goddamn-weird hunters/campers/visitors wet dreams underneath the stars. ↗

CAN I GET SOME FRIES WITH THOSE SHAKES?

Milk Shakes, originally known as *Twin Tits*, is in Columbia County, Washington.

MUST BE JAM CUZ JELLY DON'T SHAKE LIKE THAT.

The name derives from the fact that these two mountains do, in fact, look very much like extremely large breasts.

SHAKE IT UP, BABY.

Will they develop stretch marks some day in the geological future?

MINGE,
LITHUANIA

Appropriately enough, Minge is wet. If you're not sure why this is important, ask a friend from England.

Minge is a term Brits use for a woman's vagina. It's equivalent to *pussy*. In fact, some older folks in part of Northern England use *minge* as a perfectly nondirty way to denote a feline.

Minge, Lithuania really *is* wet. Its main roads are actually rivers that aren't traversed by bridges. It's often called the Lithuanian Venice. Of course, anyone with any sense would prefer to go to Venice, Italy, since Lithuania is the European equivalent of some godforsaken, hole-in-the-wall state like South Dakota or Wyoming.

The town gets its name not from hot women—this *is* Eastern Europe, after all—but from the Minija River. In fact, the town sometimes is known as *Minija*, but that's not a particularly funny name. *Minge*, on the other hand, *is* a funny name. ↗

WHERE IS MINGE?

So many possible joke answers here . . .

WHY IS IT CALLED MINGE?

Minge is a corruption of the Minija River, which flows through town.

WHAT DO YOU NEED TO KNOW ABOUT MINGE?

It is called the Lithuanian Venice.

MONKEYS EYEBROW,
KENTUCKY

Kentucky and rednecks? Check. Kentucky and moonshine? Check. Kentucky and horses? Gotcha. Kentucky and monkeys? Screech. Wait a minute . . . WTF?

Monkeys Eyebrow is a small, unincorporated community in extreme western Kentucky. Although it is near a nature preserve, no monkeys of any kind have been known to frolic in the environs. If there have been no monkeys, then— *ipso facto*—there can be no monkey eyebrows. Do monkeys even *have* eyebrows?

How in the hell did this small community in Kentucky's Ballard County get its weird name? Well, if you look at a map of the county, it does, in fact, look a little like a monkey's head . . . especially if you're pickled on moonshine.

And if the county were, in fact, a monkey's head, then Monkeys Eyebrow would be in the location of the monkey's chin, right? No, numbnuts, it would be the monkey's eyebrow, of course.

In fact, once upon a time, the area had *two* Monkeys. Old Monkey (no shit, seriously) was at the top of a hill, and New Monkey was at the bottom of the hill. Now, there is only one Monkey . . . or at least one Monkeys Eyebrow.

And, yes, genius. If you're wondering . . . these are hill people, after all. They left out the apostrophe that *should* be in the word *Monkeys*. Enjoy your millisecond of superiority. ↗

WHERE IS MONKEYS EYEBROW?

It's in Kentucky's Ballard County, or on the visages of unibrowed primates.

WHY IS IT NAMED *MONKEYS EYEBROW*?

On a map, the county looks a little like a monkey's head. Monkeys Eyebrow is right about where the monkey's eyebrow would be.

WHAT DO YOU NEED TO KNOW ABOUT MONKEYS EYEBROW?

The community has never heard of apostrophes.

MONO COUNTY,
CALIFORNIA

You *knew* that if there were a county in the United States that could give you mono, it would *have* to be located in California, where the state animal is a virus that causes some sort of venereal disease. At least this county, in the central part of the state just across the border from Nevada, only gives you mononucleosis, the so-called "kissing disease." Since you probably lived a lonely teenage existence, you may not have experienced mono. It's spread orally and causes sore throat, fever, and fatigue. It got you out of school and allowed you to make up fantastic stories about how you contracted it in the first place.

Since most pinheads find *mononucleosis* hard to spell, the California county, which must have had a mononucleosis epidemic at some point in its history, is named simply *Mono*. Folks there must spend most of their time on disability and away from work. That sucks. Oh, wait a minute. It turns out that the name is a tribute to Paiute Indians, who once ruled large portions of Nevada and California. One group had eating habits similar to yours. Their diet consisted largely of fly larvae, so other tribes, perhaps as an insult, called them *monachie*, or *fly people*. Over time, *monachie* became *Mono*.

So, um, the county has a name that sounds like a shortened form of "mononucleosis" because early residents there ate flies. You know, we're all for paying tribute to history, but . . . sometimes you just need to let it go, man. ↗

WHERE IS MONO?

Mono County is just east of the Sierra Nevada Mountains and just across the border from Nevada.

WHY IS IT NAMED *MONO*?

An early Paiute tribe in the area liked to eat maggots, so other tribes called them *monachie*, or *fly people*. *Monachie* became *Mono*.

WHAT DO YOU NEED TO KNOW ABOUT MONO?

You get it from kissing someone, so *you* don't have to worry about contracting it.

MONSTER,
HOLLAND

The Netherlands needs a quick civics lesson. A town's name should evoke pleasant associations: sunshine, joy, fidelity, strength. A town's name should *not* evoke the stuff of nightmares or a brand of energy drink.

Hmm. Maybe if the folks in the capital of Amsterdam weren't so busy getting wasted on legal pot and busting their nuts with legal prostitutes, then they would have realized that one of their country's cities is named *Monster*.

Other than potent pot, there are two reasons the town might have gained its name. Some believe Monster comes from the Latin word, *monasterium*, which means monastery. Others believe the name is derived from another Latin word, *monstrum*, which refers to a large church. Or, maybe, it's just a place people hang out in when possessing a monster buzz.

Photos of the town do not suggest anything frightening or monstrous within Monster's city limits unless one considers extreme boredom to be monstrous. There's a church and a windmill and not much else. No prostitutes. No pot. Jesus, you might as well just hang in Amsterdam. ↗

WHERE IS MONSTER?

Monster is in the province of South Holland, on the North Sea, which is *not* known to possess monsters like, say, Scotland's Loch Ness.

WHY IS IT NAMED MONSTER?

The name probably comes from a Latin word that has something to do with churches or monasteries.

WHAT DO YOU NEED TO KNOW ABOUT MONSTER?

The most frightening thing there is extreme boredom.

MOREHEAD,
KENTUCKY

Most guys have trouble reaching agreement. You know . . . one guy wants to watch the Colts. Another wants to watch the Raiders. One guy likes fancy-ass beer, while everyone else calls him "gay" and is happy with whatever's cheapest. But there is one thing all guys agree on: Morehead is good.

Yep. Once is not enough. Twice is good but insufficient. Morehead! Morehead! Must. Have. Morehead. Fortunately, there's the perfect spot for gentlemen of all stripes.

Morehead was named for former Kentucky governor, James T. Morehead. Whether or not Mr. Morehead himself received Morehead than other men of his era is lost to history. He did, however, leave his name.

Nowadays, Morehead is fairly large for a small town. It boasts about 6,000 people. Maybe its population is testament to the joys of experiencing Morehead on a regular basis. ↗

> ### WHERE IS MOREHEAD?
>
> Don't get excited. It's nowhere near *you*.

> ### WHY IS IT NAMED AFTER GETTING HEAD?
>
> Morehead is named for a former Kentucky governor, James T. Morehead. Perhaps the gentleman was a total player.

> ### WHAT DO YOU NEED TO KNOW ABOUT MOREHEAD?
>
> It was the site of a vicious feud between two families, the Underwoods and Holbrooks, during the late nineteenth century.

MORON,
ARGENTINA

We've all been accused of being a moron at some point in our lives, right? No? I'm the only one? Anyway ... there's the perfect place for all of us just South of the Border, in a place called Moron. It's true! The place is named for idiots, lunkheads, doofuses (doofi?), and your mom. Well, sort of.

Moron is a Romance Language salad that means "hillock of the Earth." Thus, people in this section of Buenos Aires are proud to be Morons. In fact, they've been Morons for over 500 years. Visit today, and you'll be surrounded by more than 300,000 Morons.

Imagine it! You can attend the Universidad de Moron (Moron University!!) or spend your time chasing Moronic pursuits. ➚

WHERE IS IT, YOU MORON?

Moron is part of the Argentine province of Buenos Aires.

WHY IS IT CALLED MORON?

Moron loosely translates to "hillock of the Earth."

WHAT DO YOU NEED TO KNOW ABOUT MORON?

The city contains more than 300,000 Morons, at least some of whom attend Moron University.

MOUND,
LOUISIANA

First off, this town should be Mounds. Then it would suggest breasts. After all, it's named for the presence of Indian burial mounds in the community. Surely, there's more than one. What's the matter with these people? Couldn't they have gone for the obvious play on words? Oh well, one Mound is better than no Mound at all, we guess.

This particular Mound is small. It's got about a dozen residents. Perhaps few live in the community because its name has sexual overtones and, in the heart of the Deep South, sex is bad, m'kay? Or, more likely, few people live there because they'd rather live almost *any* place other than this Podunk little town just across the border from Alabama. ↗

WHERE IS MOUND?

Mound is in Louisiana's Madison Parish. In Louisiana, counties are called *parishes* for some stupid reason.

WHY IS IT CALLED MOUND?

It is located around a lot of Indian burial mounds.

WHAT DO YOU NEED TO KNOW ABOUT MOUND?

Its name would be funnier if it were *Mounds*.

MOUNT DICK,
NEW ZEALAND

Now, that's a big Dick. Really. It's huge. It sticks up nearly a half-mile. Makes you feel like you've got plankton between your legs, doesn't it?

Mount Dick stands splendidly erect atop New Zealand's Adams Island, one of the largest in that country's Auckland Islands chain. And while it's possible the peak was named by an explorer with extreme delusions of self-grandeur, Mount Dick most likely was named for R.G. Dick, onetime surveyor general of New Zealand, or to honor a nine-teenth century politician, Thomas Dick.

It's not known if Mr. Dick carried an armadillo in his trousers or was, instead, of average endowment. He kept a diary but apparently neglected to touch on this seminal fact.

If you visit Mount Dick, it's not your johnson you've got to watch out for; it's your balls because they might freeze right off in this Subantarctic portion of New Zealand. You might even be able to see Antarctica from the head of Mount Dick.

One note of caution: If you're hoping to score near Mount Dick, keep in mind it's nowhere near any permanent settlements. No people, just the occasional sheep. ↗

WHERE IS THIS BIG DICK?

Mount Dick stands massively erect and engorged on New Zealand's Subantarctic Auckland Islands.

HOW DID THE BIG DICK GET ITS NAME?

Most likely, Mount Dick was named in honor of nineteenth-century New Zealand politician, Thomas Dick.

WHAT DO I NEED TO KNOW ABOUT THIS BIG DICK?

Mount Dick is 2,300-feet tall when fully erect, and it was once the rim of a now-extinct volcano. Some sort of joke about Cialis seems appropriate here . . .

MOUNT FAGET,
ANTARCTICA

Can't you just imagine the clever, frat house, Antarctican humor about this next place? *Hey, dude. They named a mountain after you! It's pretty impressive. It's, like, 4,000 meters tall. You ought to go down and claim it. Take some of your friends. I'm sure they'll be more than happy to accompany you to Mount Faget.*

Forget about trying to claim it's pronounced "fah-jay" or something. Anyone who knows you knows you're always eager to Mount Faget. No offense, bro. I mean, there's nothing wrong with that really. Just, you know, don't get too close to me in the locker room or anything.

Nah, seriously, bro. Real talk for a second. Mount Faget was named for Maxime A. Faget of the National Aeronautics and Space Administration. That's NASA, numbnuts. She visited McMurdo Station in 1966. That's an American research center located on Ross Island. Turns out it's got, like, 1,258 people. It's the most populated spot on Antarctica.

So, you know, after you've had a chance to Mount Faget, you can head to McMurdo and, like, get a Swedish massage or something. From a guy. Ha! Later, bro. ↗

WHERE IS MOUNT FAGET?

It's in Antarctica. Where in Antarctica? Shit, who knows? There's nothing *in* Antarctica except mountains and penguins.

WHY IS IT NAMED *FAGET*?

The mountain was named for a former official with NASA.

WHAT DO YOU NEED TO KNOW ABOUT MOUNT FAGET?

Maybe you can tell us a thing or two.

MOUNT MEE,
AUSTRALIA

There's a community in Australia that has, at its doorstep, the perfect hook for world travelers like yourself: "Feeling horny? Mount Mee!" Why the hell isn't this Queensland suburb taking advantage of this slogan? They must be ass-backwards.

The original name for this forested Australian paradise was *Dahmonga*, an indigenous word for "flying squirrel." Once European settlers arrived, they took a local term for "lookout" — *mia-mia* — and adapted it slightly to *Mee*.

Mount Mee residents go about their daily lives — shopping, polishing their cars, mounting each other like wildebeests — while surrounded by a state forest that provides plenty of protective cover for four-legged and two-legged creatures trying to do what comes naturally.

So, remember . . . feeling horny? Mount Mee! ↗

WHERE CAN YOU MOUNT MEE?

Mount Mee is a community in Queensland. Maybe this is why Queensland is known as the *Smart State* of Australia.

WHY MOUNT MEE?

Because you're available, I've been drinking, I haven't had any in a really long time . . .

WHAT DO YOU NEED TO MOUNT MEE?

A few hundred bucks. Oh, who am I kidding. I'll pay *you*.

MUCKLE FLUGGA,
SCOTLAND

Admittedly, the original name for the British Isles' penultimate northern point wasn't, shall we say, aesthetically pleasing. *North Unst* is akin to a sound you'd make as you're about to puke up a pint of Everclear: wretch, hurl, unst. So, it makes sense the powers that be would change the name of this small island.

But here's the new name, adopted in 1964: Muckle Flugga. There's just something inherently silly about those syllables. *Muckle Flugga* sounds like a character you'd find on *Yo Gabba Gabba!* or some other surrealistic children's show. Leave it to the Brits; they *do* love their silliness.

The island's name is slightly amended from the Old Norse phrase, *mikla flugey*, which means "I'm about to hawk up a nasty loogie on you" or, possibly, "large, steep-sided island."

According to legend, the islands were formed when two giants fought over the same mermaid. The horny giants threw huge rocks at each other, one of which became Muckle Flugga. Nowadays, the island is known for its scenic beauty, its lighthouse, and its ridiculous name. ↗

WHERE IS MUCKLE FLUGGA?

Muckle Flugga is about as far north as one can go and still be on part of Great Britain.

WHY IS IT NAMED *MUCKLE FLUGGA*?

Because Scottish folks can't spell *motherfucker*?!?

WHAT DO YOU NEED TO KNOW ABOUT MUCKLE FLUGGA?

The island was formed when giants fought over a mermaid, which raises the question: How could giants have sex with a mermaid anyway?

MUFF,
IRELAND

There's only one problem with Muff. It's always wet! Sometimes it's just damp. Sometimes it's fully saturated. But if wet Muff bothers you, then you might find a place like Dix, Nebraska (see page 66) more to your liking.

Muff is an Anglicized version of the Gaelic word, *magh*, which means field or plain. That's the official explanation, anyway. But some folks in the community are happy to engage in the double entendre business. If you want to take up scuba while visiting Eire, then head over to Muff Divers and suit up!

In recent years, the population of Muff has exploded. Could it be due to folks who don't understand the etymology of the town's name? Thousands of horny, lonely guys (sound familiar?) crossing over from Northern Ireland to get some.

Every year, Muff celebrates the Muff Festival. Unfortunately, it's not what you might envision in your fantasies. It's just your standard music, food, booze, and fun sort of fracas. But, you never know, you could get lucky. Then, for the rest of your (mostly alone) days, you can talk about how you got some muff in Muff. ↗

WHERE CAN I GET SOME MUFF?

Muff, Ireland is in Ireland's County Donegal, just like another oddly named place: Raphoe (see page 157).

I NEED SOME MUFF.

Muff comes from *magh*, a Gaelic words that means "pussy." Oh, wait. No, it means "field" or "plain."

COME SEE MUFF.

While in Muff, enjoy the Muff Festival. Or enjoy Muff Divers!

MYSTERY SPOT,
SANTA CRUZ, CALIFORNIA

Dude, people have, like, totally been staggering around portions of California at least since Owsley Stanley began to work his magic in the 1960s. But there's one place that drug-addled behavior and glimmering visions are perfectly natural: Santa Cruz's Mystery Spot.

Due, some believe (yes, they *really* believe this . . . hey, it *is* California), to a buried alien spaceship, there is a 150-foot-in-diameter spot in Santa Cruz where the laws of physics and gravity are turned on their heads, leaving you feeling like you're enduring a bad trip or at least a brutal hangover.

Inside a house on the property, rubber balls seem to roll uphill, chairs can sit upright on walls, people can stay on their feet while leaning over to a disturbing degree, and some folks actually believe Lady Gaga is talented.

The Mystery Spot claims these anomalies are real, but the mystery most likely is nothing more than the fact that the house is slanted some twenty degrees, fooling the mind into thinking that uphill is downhill, level is slanted, and that there's artistic merit to most Seth Rogen films. ↗

JINKIES, WHERE IS THIS MYSTERY?

The Mystery Spot was located by some men about three miles from Santa Cruz . . . not to be confused with the G-spot, which no man has ever been able to locate.

JINKIES, WHY IS THE MYSTERY SPOT?

On this site, gravity and physics are supposed to go haywire. Visiting the Mystery Spot while on hallucinogenics is *not* recommended.

JINKIES, WHAT DO YOU NEED TO KNOW ABOUT THIS MYSTERY?

Most likely, "mystery spots" like this one are due to optical illusions . . . or to some totally bitchin' acid.

NO NAME,
COLORADO

The next time you're driving down Interstate 70 in Colorado, keep your ears open for variations of the following conversation...

"What's the name of the town at that next exit?"

"No name."

"Don't be an asshole. What's its name?"

"No Name."

"Listen, if you don't tell me what the fuck that town is named right now, I'm gonna kick your ass."

"The name of the town is *No Name*."

"Bullshit! Oh, yeah . . . you're right. It's right there on the sign . . . ."

No Name exists due to Interstate 70. When the interstate was being built and exits planned, surveyors planned an exit for a community that didn't have a name. Just as a place holder, so to speak, the surveyors designated the area around the ramp "No Name."

Time went by, the interstate ramp was finished, and folks started moving into the small, unincorporated community. Coloradoans, being a rather simpleminded lot, became proud of telling folks that they "lived in No Name."

Eventually, the so-called powers-that-be attempted to give the community a proper name. Locals wouldn't hear of it. They fought city hall and won, so the town remains No Name. You can catch a glimpse of the exit sign in the 1971 grindhouse classic, *Vanishing Point.* ⏎

WHERE IS NO NAME?

It's just east of Glenwood Springs, off Interstate 70.

WHY IS IT NAMED *NO NAME*?

Surveyors realized this area along the proposed interstate lacked a name and simply called it *No Name*. Folks in the area decided they liked being No Name and fought efforts to give the place a real name.

WHAT DO YOU NEED TO KNOW ABOUT NO NAME?

You can catch a glimpse of the interstate sign in an old movie called *Vanishing Point*.

NORMAL,
ILLINOIS

You would think a place featuring a large university would encourage uniqueness. But, no. You'd better not fuck around in Normal. Do everything the way you're supposed to do it.

Follow all the rules. Don't make waves. Look, act, sing, pee, whatever just like everybody else. In a word: Be normal (well, that's two words, but you know what we mean).

How did this place get to be so, well, normal? Ironically, it was the university's fault. Once upon a time, the city was named North Bloomington. It was the site of Illinois State Normal University. A "normal" university is one that trains teachers.

Anywho, over time the school lent its name to the town, but then the university pulled a cruel trick, changing its name to Illinois State University.

Now, all these Normal people are walking around—toeing the line, following all traffic laws no matter how insignificant, staying married, having 2.3 children. And they have a Normal place to eat as well. The original Steak 'n Shake restaurant opened in Normal in 1934. ↗

WHERE IS NORMAL?

Normal is just north of Bloomington, Illinois. It's the site of Illinois State University.

WHY BE NORMAL?

A "normal" school trains teachers. Illinois State University was once known as Illinois State Normal University.

WHAT DO YOU NEED TO KNOW ABOUT NORMAL?

Don't be fooled. These people are *not* normal. They are total freaks.

NOTHING,
ARIZONA

If you've thought to yourself that some of the names in this book must have come from the mouths of drunks, then you are basically incorrect . . . until now. Finally! There *is* a town in Arizona that is happy to claim it was originated by a group of drunken reprobates.

Or were these worldly philosophers? After all, Mohave County is pretty much the middle of nowhere. What are you going to find there? Nothing. Ah! It all makes sense.

For years, the town's entrance sign tried to be philosophical. It claimed that the town's name was a result of the fact that its citizens (all four of them) "had faith in Nothing, hoped for Nothing, [and] worked at Nothing, for Nothing."

Nothing's sole business was a gas station, built around 1977 when the town was founded. The gas station was abandoned in 2005 and began to return to dust by 2008. But all is not lost in Nothing!

An eatery has been established in Nothing, and the town's owner, Mike Jensen, has plans to create some sort of renaissance in a town named for absolutely Nothing. What are our expectations? Nothing. ↗

WHERE IS NOTHING?

Nothing is in Mohave County, Arizona, which basically means it is, in fact, Nothing surrounded by nothing.

WHY IS IT NAMED *NOTHING*?

Drunken residents named the town, according to legend.

WHAT DO YOU NEED TO KNOW ABOUT NOTHING?

Nothing.

ODD,
WEST VIRGINIA

West Virginia is odd to start with. It's one of two states that basically owes its existence to the Civil War (Nevada is the other). It's known as the state that helped JFK get elected to the presidency, probably with a lot of help from organized crime. And it's filled with inhospitable landscapes littered with crumbling mines.

Therefore, is it a wonder that such an odd state would have within its borders a city actually *named Odd*? Shit no! And, as you might expect, the name exists because of people who did not have their shit together.

Long ago, people in the fledgling community gathered at the local post office to come up with a name for their new town. Folks threw out all kinds of names, which have since been lost to history. Apparently, though, one of the names was particularly bizarre. Perhaps it was French Lick or Toad Suck or Crapo (see pages 82, 175, and 48).

The story goes that, upon hearing this bizarre name, someone in the post office said, "That's odd" or "How odd" or something along those lines. Before you could say "Big Bone Lick State Park"(see page 17), the town's name officially was *Odd*. And Odd it remains. ⏎

WHERE IS ODD?

It's in Raleigh County, along the banks of Tommy Creek.

WHY IS IT SO ODD?

When the town was being named, residents couldn't agree on a name. The consensus was that anything was fine so long as it was odd.

WHAT DO YOU NEED TO KNOW ABOUT ODD?

It contained the last wooden school house used in West Virginia. The school was used until 1989.

ORAL,
SOUTH DAKOTA

Since there does not appear to be a town in the United States named *Blow Job*, we have combed the map to find the next best thing: a town called *Oral*. True, there are some nonsexual uses of the word *oral*. For example, a televangelist with that name once claimed God would kill him unless he managed to bilk followers out of eight million dollars. Also, if one is a dentist or dental hygienist, one probably gets used to the word *oral* being thrown around like so much bloody gum tissue.

But for most of us, *Oral* conjures up pictures of oral sex, as in, "Hey, dude. I totally just got some oral from Jane." So, if you're looking for a place where you're *guaranteed* to find some Oral, then head (pun intended) north, way north, to South Dakota. There, you will find an entire town focused on Oral.

Locals will tell you that, most likely, the town was named for the son of the community's first postmaster. But that's total bullshit. The town was named Oral because it is filled with freaky people who are so bored—due to choosing a life in a godforsaken state like South Dakota—that all they do is sit around, drink shitty beer, and get off on Oral.

If this sounds like the life of which you've been dreaming, then head (pun intended) north, my friend. ↗

> **WHERE IS ORAL?**
> You can find Oral in Fall River County. Just look for the Oral Fire Department.

> **WHY IS IT NAMED AFTER A BLOW JOB?**
> In fact, it is likely named for a son of the community's first postmaster.

> **WHAT DO YOU NEED TO KNOW ABOUT ORAL?**
> It feels good and will not cause pregnancy.

PECULIAR,
MISSOURI

All the folks in Peculiar have something, well, odd about them. Some have extra limbs. Some are giants. Some are dwarves. You might find a stray pinhead or two, if you look carefully. Yep, there's a good reason this town is named *Peculiar*. Actually, the only thing peculiar about Peculiar is that there is nothing particularly interesting, much less peculiar, about the community. Like some other towns in this book, Peculiar owes its name to the burgeoning community having its collective thumb up its metaphorical ass.

Folks in the new town were having a difficult time coming up with an appropriate name for their new burg. They narrowed the possibilities down to a handful of choices, but Knob Lick was already taken (see page 114). Okay, they didn't really consider Knob Lick, but all of the citizens' names really were in use elsewhere in the state.

When the region's postmaster told the disappointed citizens of the as-yet-to-be-named town that they were SOL (shit outta luck), the citizens threw up their hands, uttered a collective "fuck it," and told the postmaster that any name would do as long as it were peculiar.

This guy's response? Hey, why don't you just name the town "Peculiar" and be done with it? He probably was joking, but folks in Missouri are not known for their brilliance, so either they took him at his word or their brains were hurting from thinking up new town names. Peculiar it became. Peculiar it remains. ↗

WHERE IS PECULIAR?

It's in Cass County, adjacent to the Kansas border.

WHY IS IT *PECULIAR*?

For the same reason Odd is *Odd* (see page 150). Folks couldn't decide on a name and declared anything would be fine, as long as it was kind of peculiar.

WHAT DO YOU NEED TO KNOW ABOUT PECULIAR?

If you look at the city's website, the community appears to be sort of sensitive about being thought of as "peculiar." Tough break.

PEE PEE,

OHIO

Jesus Christ. You just can't make stuff like this up. Yes, there is a town in the United States named *Pee Pee*, as in piss, piddle, miterate, number one. How, you might ask, did this come to be? Was the town stumbled upon, or, rather, pissed upon by accident? Was it named by the founder's two-year-old? Do the folks there just like to celebrate a good stint of urination?

Nope, nope, and nope. Apparently, the town is named for the Pee Pee River. Why did anyone think to name a river after pee pee? It seems that the river was discovered in the eighteenth century by an Irish settler whose initials were . . . you guessed it . . . P. P.

Now, *that* explains the origin of the name, but it does *not* explain why the folks in town decided that *Pee Pee* would make a good name for their fledgling town. What business in its right mind would want to relocate to beautiful, downtown Pee Pee? What tourists, other than the jejune sort who might read books like this one, would want to vacation deep in Pee Pee?

Granted, the town was formed in 1798, at a time when, one imagines, people's sense of humor was much less juvenile. Perhaps it did not occur to them that, some years later, people would wet themselves when hearing of a town named Pee Pee.

Nowadays, the community is home to some 8,000 souls, all of whom are proud to say they come from Pee Pee. ↗

> **WHERE IS PEE PEE?**
>
> On and around the toilet if your aim sucks.

> **WHY IS IT NAMED *PEE PEE*?**
>
> A local river, the Pee Pee, was apparently named for the initials of an Irishman who discovered it. The town that grew up around the river also became Pee Pee.

> **WHAT DO YOU NEED TO KNOW ABOUT PEE PEE?**
>
> So many possible joke answers, it's hard to settle on just one!

PHUKET,
THAILAND

Ah, fuck it. Jewel of the Far East, site of favorite Asian beaches, and home to almost-legal prostitution.

Sadly, it's pronounced "POO-ket." Anyway, it's a pretty nice place: sandy, white beaches covering much of its 350 square miles; friendly, peace-loving Buddhist natives; and, oh yeah, a sex trade that would make 1970s-era Times Square blush. Supposedly, the authorities in Phuket will look the other way, but we are in no way, shape, or form liable for any choices you make while sporting beer goggles.

But this is *not* why the city carries its salacious appellation. *Phuket* is a variation of the Malay word, *bukit*, which means "hill." From the surrounding Andaman Sea, Phuket looks like a large hill . . . or like an engorged penis that makes up in tremendous girth what it lacks in disappointing length.

Oh, and while you're in the area, don't forget to visit a nearby island chain notable for snorkeling and diving opportunities: the Phi Phi (PEE PEE) Islands. Just don't drink the water! ↗

WHERE THE PHUK IS IT?

Phuket is a province in southern Thailand. It takes up 350 square miles. That's a lot of room for nearly legal prostitution.

HOW THE PHUKET DID IT GET ITS NAME?

Phuket derives from *bukit*, a Malay word that means "hill." Phuket is a very mountainous island, so get off your dead ass and exercise before you get there.

WHAT THE PHUKET DO YOU NEED TO KNOW ABOUT IT?

Phuket first thrived due to the tin industry, but for the last several decades it has become popular for its beaches. Most of its inhabitants are Buddhist, while roughly a third are Muslim. Did we mention the active sex trade?

PIPPA PASSES,
KENTUCKY

If you go to Westminster Cathedral's Poets' Corner, you may detect an odd sound emanating from the grave of Robert Browning. Listen? Do you hear it? It's the sound of the famous narrative poet spinning wildly in his grave, horrified to know that one of his most famous poems has been claimed by a small town in Kentucky best known for moonshine and inbreeding.

Since you slept through English class, we'll remind you that "Pippa Passes" is a poem about a girl who works in a sweatshop. It contains the famous line, "God's in His heaven. All's right with the world." But not all's right in Pippa Passes, Kentucky.

In addition to the aforementioned inbreeding, the town also has people so scared of fancy book larnin' that they refuse to call the town by its proper name. Most locals still call it Caney Creek because that ain't so damn fancy, college boy.

The town owes its official, literary name to the Browning Society. Alice Lloyd, founder of the community's small college which bears her name, solicited donations from the society for the college and for a local post office. The society, apparently not realizing that Kentucky is a cesspool of culture, suggested Pippa Passes for the name of the post office, which, by association, became the name of the community.

Actually, not ALL residents of Pippa Passes hate poetry. Some in the town are agitating to change "Caney Creek" to "There One Was a Man from Nantucket." ↗

WHERE WILL YOU PASS PIPPA PASSES?

It's in Knott County, Kentucky.

HOW DID MY PIPPA PASSES GET ITS NAME?

It resulted from local fundraising efforts that involved the Browning Society. "Pippa Passes" is a verse drama by Robert Browning.

WHAT DO YOU NEED TO KNOW ABOUT PIPPA PASSES?

Most locals still call it by its old, original name: Caney Creek.

PUSSY,
FRANCE

France is *the* place to go when you want to find Pussy. Yeah, yeah, you can always opt for a Parisian whore, but you *should* be able to get it for free if you visit the small village of Pussy.

The name is a Latin/French bastardization of the word *pusus,* which means "little boy," and despite the sexiness of its name, Pussy's population has been shrinking steadily since the sixteenth century. At that time, there were over 1,400 Pussyites? Pussyians? Pussy Hounds? As of now, France's Pussy is home to fewer than 300 people.

It's a pretty big Pussy, covering some seven square miles. The local church is named in honor of St. John the Baptist, appropriate since he was the poor schmuck beheaded because King Herod couldn't get enough pussy from that hussy, Salome. ⏎

CAN YOU HELP ME FIND MY PUSSY?
Sure, it's near the Alps in southeastern France.

HOW DID MY PUSSY GET ITS NAME?
Pussy derives from the Gallo-Roman word meaning "little boy," which suggests some sort of Michael Jackson joke except that he's dead and that would be really mean.

WHAT DO YOU NEED TO KNOW ABOUT PUSSY?
It is near Mont Bellachat. It is near the River Isere. It is near the clitoris.

RAPHOE,
IRELAND

The name looks like something a pimp or Young Jeezy would do to a young lady not meeting with his expectations. He'd reach back and *slam*. Take that, hoe! But the name is actually pronounced in that combination of poetry and vowel-laden-heaviness that makes Gaelic (pronounced like something consenting gay people do to each other) such a beautiful language.

Raphoe is in Ireland's County Donegal, one of the northernmost in the country. The name is some sort of mongrelization of *Rath Bhoth*, which means "Umma slap my bitch around" in English. All right, it actually means "fort" and "hut" and probably comes from structures built by monks who settled in the area back in the far reaches of history.

The monks built clay and wattle (whatever the fuck *that* is) huts and surrounded them with fortified mounds because these weren't, like, Shaolin monks who could beat your—or your hoe's—ass if given half a chance.

Religion has always been an important part of Raphoe's culture. The town is home to the Beltany stone circle, a sort-of bargain-basement Stonehenge that's probably close to the same age as England's better-known circle of giant rocks. ↗

PIMPIN' AIN'T EASY, SO RAPHOE.

Raphoe is in Ireland's agriculturally rich County Donegal.

YO, YO, YO, RAPHOE.

Raphoe is a contraction of Gaelic words that mean "hut" and "fort" because of ancient hoe-beating monks who built huts and forts in the area a really, really long time ago.

RAPHOE ON THIS.

Raphoe is home to the remains of the "Bishop's Palace," a castle laid siege to during the Irish Rebellion of 1641, during which many hoes were rapped.

ROCK CITY,
TENNESSEE

The folks at Rock City, near Chattanooga, claim you can stand on lover's leap and see seven states. Most likely, you can see three or four, but who is going to visit a tourist attraction that allows you to "see three states"? Rock City should ignore the stupid "see seven states" garbage. The coolest thing about this bizarre monument to . . . rocks and gnomes is the gnomes! Go through the various caves of this tourist trap, and you'll find giant garden gnomes cavorting. Some are making moonshine. Some are mining for jewels.

Rock City, which has advertisements painted on nearly 1,000 barns throughout the Southeast, was created in the 1920s by Garnet and Frieda Carter, who also invented miniature golf. At first, the couple capitalized on the all the weird-looking rock formations found on the property, which sits atop Lookout Mountain. Over time, however, the couple realized—long before the 1960s—that people love to go on acid trips. Therefore, they placed DayGlo gnomes in various places, but then they added the *piece de resistance*: Fairyland Caverns.

Fairyland Caverns is just far enough underground to make your head spin a little bit, and when you see a black-lit fairyland populated with nursery rhyme characters—a grinning Humpty Dumpty, a sadistic Jack Sprat, a recalcitrant Little Jack Horner—you will feel like you got a double dose of Sunshine or Windowpane dropped onto your tongue. ↗

WHERE IS ROCK CITY?

Technically just over the Georgia border, most consider Rock City part of Chattanooga, Tennessee.

WTF IS IT?

Rock City has a bunch of rocks, a vantage point from which one supposedly can see seven states, and all kinds of psychedelic gnomes and Day-Glo nursery rhyme characters.

WHAT DO YOU NEED TO KNOW ABOUT ROCK CITY?

Do not *actually* drop acid before visiting, or your mind will wind up completely and unalterably fucked.

SASMU...
(FORMERLY SE...)
PHILIPPINES

God, Philippines, what is the matter wi[...]
we're not talking about your part in the [...]
American War, the Bataan Death March, [...]
Imelda Marcos's love of shoes. You guys ha[...]
with the coolest name *ever*, and you got rid [...]

Sasmuan. Okay, it sounds all tribal and ev[...]ing,
but for hundreds of years, you guys were *Sexmoan*.
God, how many horny college students over the
years do you think flocked to your little archipelago
because it sounded like you had the hottest sex tourism in the entire freaking world?

Sexmoan became *Sasmuan* in 1987 for two reasons. The first was historical, the second hysterical.
Sasmuan was the city's original name, a mishmash of
Polynesian languages that meant, in essence, "meeting place of courageous men." Spanish conquistadors
took the name and garbled it further, into *Sexmoan*.
And Sexmoan it stood, for a few hundred years. The
community is going back to its roots by renaming
itself Sasmuan.

The other reason? People thought *Sexmoan* was
a funny name. Although locally the town's name was
not pronounced "SEX MOAN," that's how folks from
the West pronounced it. So, Sexmoan reclaimed its
original spelling and, *voila*, no more laughter from
capitalist pigs . . . and no more visits from horny capitalist teenagers, either. ↗

[...] people,
[...]d on Manila
Bay.

WHY WAS IT SEXMOAN?

Sexmoan was a cor-
ruption of the town's
original name, Sas-
muan, bequeathed
to the community
by Spanish conquis-
tadors. *Sexmoan/
Sasmuan* means
"meeting place of
courageous men." In
modern times, the
name *Sexmoan*
became an embar-
rassment, so the city
changed its name to
the original spelling.

WHAT DO YOU NEED TO KNOW ABOUT SEXMOAN?

No matter how realis-
tic it sounds, she still
may be faking it.

...g now, or shall we shag later? If you live ...ealand you've got not one, but *two* places ...re guaranteed to find a shag. In fact, you'll find hundreds of shags. Just think of it. And no, we're not talking about a kind of dancing done near the beach in the southeastern United States. Yes, they shag there, but it's just a dance . . . not even dirty dancing, just dancing. In New Zealand, you can find honest-to-God shags.

Shag Island, also known as Tarahiki Island, is in New Zealand's Hauraki Gulf, about twenty miles from the mainland. People flock to the island because of all the available shags. Folks whip out their cameras to take pictures of all the shags.

All those shags are how the island got its name. Shag Island is home to a breeding colony of more than 700 spotted shags. A spotted shag is not some new kind of kinky sex. It's a bird, a species of cormorant.

Shag Island is not far from Shag Reef, which also earned its name thanks to all those feathery shags. So, we're afraid you will have to continue to be a wanker . . . even if you go to Shag Island. ↗

WHERE IS SHAG ISLAND?

It's off the coast of New Zealand.

WHY IS IT CALLED SHAG ISLAND?

Because it has a lot of shags. Duh!

WHAT DO YOU NEED TO KNOW ABOUT SHAG ISLAND?

What the fuck is a cormorant?

SHITTERTON,
ENGLAND

You think *your* job sucks? Imagine being the poor schmuck who's trying to sell property in Shitterton, a community in England's Dorset County. Sure, Shitterton is in a beautiful region made famous by Thomas Hardy—though I don't believe he ever mentioned this particular hamlet—but ... well, it's actually named after shit.

Most likely, *Shitterton* is named in honor (if you can call it an honor) of a nearby stream that was used as a ... well, as a shitter by animals and people alike in the millennia prior to indoor plumbing.

Shitterton has some 2,000 Shittertonians? Shittertonites? Many of them surely have developed a sense of humor about their hometown. But not everyone laughs in the face of shit. Some locals try unobtrusively to remove the "h" from their town's name, but, to no avail.

For now, Shitterton remains. ⬈

EXCUSE ME. WHERE IS THE SHITTER?

Shitterton is a small community in England's Dorset County.

WHY THE SHITTY NAME?

Once upon a time, people and animals pooped in a town stream.

HOLY SHITTERTON!

Shitterton actually is named for poo poo.

SHOW LOW,
ARIZONA

No, it's not a command for a bashful pole dancer. Show Low, Arizona is named for the manner in which the town was founded. It was not won by an epic battle with Native Americans nor through the efforts of hardy pioneers. Instead, it was won by a card game.

In the nineteenth century, two men—C.E. Cooley and Marion Clark—took a trite Western film cliché and made it reality. They decided a 100,000 acre ranch was not big enough for the both of them. Apparently big pussies, Cooley and Clark did not resort to a duel or to fisticuffs in order to claim the ranch. They opted for a card game.

One of the two allegedly said that whoever drew the lowest card could have the ranch. Cooley turned up the deuce of clubs—considered the lowest-ranking card in the deck—and won. To this day, Show Low's main street is named Deuce of Clubs in tribute.

Nowadays, there's not much to Show Low except for some extremely fucked up weather. Since the community sits more than a mile above sea level, it tends to hit freezing temperatures at least once during every month except for July and August. At the same time, the town can achieve temperatures above one hundred degrees Fahrenheit.

You know what? You can keep the town. We'll just go to the nearest club for exotic dancers and ask *them* to Show Low. ↗

WHERE IS SHOW LOW?

Show Low is in Arizona's Navajo County.

WHY IS IT NAMED *SHOW LOW*?

The town was won by a card game. The winner had to "show low," i.e., have the lowest card.

WHAT DO YOU NEED TO KNOW ABOUT SHOW LOW?

It has extreme temperatures that are more unpredictable than a woman with PMS who can't get access to a chocolate bar.

SILLY,
BELGIUM

No place in all the world can claim to be sillier than one tiny town in the Walloon, or French-dominant, region of Belgium. We're talking zanier than Jerry Lewis's entire *oeuvre*, more madcap than drunken American frat guys using pidgin French to try and score some strange on the streets of Paris, wackier even than a badly dubbed copy of *Deuce Bigalow: European Gigolo*. Ladies and gentlemen, welcome to Silly.

The name of the town is a variation of the stream that runs through town, called the *Sille* in French and the *Zulle* in Dutch. So, alas, the Belgian municipality of about 8,000 residents isn't silly at all.

Nonetheless, it's tons of fun to go to the city's website and find such enthusiastic and jingoistic statements (in fun-filled French!) as "I am very happy to welcome you to Silly" and "The community of Silly is particularly dynamic from cultural points of view." How could it not be? ↗

STOP BEING SO FUCKING SILLY!

Silly is in the French-dominant Walloon region of northern Belgium.

WIPE THAT SILLY GRIN OFF YOUR FACE.

Silly is not named after goofiness. It's a variation of the name of the stream that runs through the town.

WHAT'S SO SILLY ABOUT IT?

Silly is particularly dynamic from cultural points of view.

SODDY-DAISY,
TENNESSEE

The name of this community near Chattanooga is, just on the face of it, silly. To truly appreciate it, though, you must be British. Then, you would know that *sod* is a kinder way to say *fuck*. As in, "Sod off, you wanker."

A *wanker* is, like you, someone who masturbates frequently because he cannot find willing female companionship. If you are, in fact, a wanker, then be sure to visit Wanker's Corner, Oregon (see page 187).

But we digress. If you understand British slang, then you would know that the town appears, like Humptulips (see page 105), to advocate sex with plant life. Hey, maybe that would be a solution for you, you pathetic freak.

There are two stories related to the "Soddy" part of this bedroom community's name. The first is that it is an English corruption of an Indian word, *tsati*, which means "sipping place." Sipping place? Oh well. Anyway, the other story is that immigrants mispronounced William Sodder's trading post as *soddy*.

Daisy was a nearby community named for Daisy Parks, daughter of a coal company president. The two communities merged and were incorporated in 1969, and Daisies have been Sodded ever since. ↗

WHERE IS SODDY-DAISY?

Soddy-Daisy is very close to Chattanooga, home of tourist traps like Rock City and Forbidden Caverns.

WHY IS IT NAMED AFTER SEX WITH FLOWERS?

Soddy may be an English corruption of an Indian word, *tsati*, which means "sipping place." *Daisy* was named for the daughter of a coal company president. The towns later merged.

WHAT DO YOU NEED TO KNOW ABOUT SODDY-DAISY?

If you're American, the name will just be silly. If you're British, you'll find the name sodding hilarious.

SOUTH OF THE BORDER,
DILLON, SOUTH CAROLINA

Mexican border towns can be tons of fun: widespread prostitution, drinking for all ages, black velvet art. Of course, they also have the downside of occasionally harboring drug cartels that like to shoot at each other in public places.

If you've ever wanted to visit a Mexican border town but were concerned about such minor travel disruptions as warring drug gangs and shitloads of drunken, obnoxious, underage Americans taking advantage of lax carding policies, then we've got just the place for you!

South of the Border is a Mexican-themed tourist trap near Dillon, South Carolina. Founder Alan Schafer got his inspiration from the fact that his place is just inches from the border of North Carolina. Get it? South of the (North Carolina) Border!

Yes, it's a lame premise, but the place is actually pretty cool . . . if you're into "shabby chic."

Take a ride up a space needle topped by a giant sombrero and gaze out over . . . absolutely nothing. Well, maybe a cow or something. Eat inside a giant sombrero. Buy snowdomes, souvenir spoons, cedar boxes, and any other piece of tourist garbage you can name.

South of the Border makes no pretense at being politically correct, but so what? Neither do you! So enjoy mascot Pedro's *hoz-pee-tal-ih-tee*, drink a bunch of Coronas, and vomit from the top of the sombrero tower! ⏎

WHERE EEZ SOUTH OF THE BORDER?

It's in Dillon, South Carolina, just south of the North Carolina border.

WHY EEZ IT SOUTH OF THE BORDER?

I just told you, numbnuts.

WHAT DOES JUAN NEED TO KNOW ABOUT SOUTH OF THE BORDER?

It's a tourist trap that spans a highway and contains tons of junk, most of which, ironically, is made in China . . . not in Mexico.

(165)

SPLOTT,
WALES

Some place names are sexy. Some are silly. Some are beautiful, putting one in mind of pleasant valleys or majestic vistas. And some places have names that evoke the sound of a can of SPAM being poured out onto a plate in front of eager youngsters. The district of Splott, in Wales, is one of these.

Locals will tell you that *Splott* is a contraction of *God's Plot*, a reference to the fact that much of the land in the district once belonged to a medieval bishop. Others might argue that the name is a variation of *plat*, which means "grassy land." But the most likely reason for the area's onomatopoeia-rich name is that it is a variation of the English word, *splot*, which means "a plot of land." Somehow, that extra "t" just makes the name sound even sillier and more like a bowel movement or the aforementioned SPAM.

Splott is part of the Welsh capital, Cardiff. Cardiff is a major port and has about 350,000 people. *Cardiff* is a nice name, one of those that sounds like a pleasant valley, while *Splott* sounds like the noise made by a shart. ↗

X MARKS THE SPLOTT

Splott is a district of Cardiff, the capital of Wales.

SPLOTT'S IN A NAME?

Splott could be a contraction of *God's Plot*, but, most likely, it is a variation of an English word meaning "parcel of land."

SPLOTT DO YOU NEED TO KNOW ABOUT SPLOTT?

It has a butt-ugly name.

SPREAD EAGLE,
WISCONSIN

They go buck wild in Wisconsin, boy. No, we're not talking about cheeseheads or Jeffrey Dahmer's exploits in Milwaukee. We're talking about the place where you can find all those Spread Eagle ladies. Just picture it: hot young things, MILFs, silver foxes, all Spread Eagle and waiting for company . . . Dang . . . the mind reels.

Of course, locals will claim that *Spread Eagle* is not a reference to the missionary position. They will claim, instead, that this unincorporated village was named for a nearby chain of lakes that, when viewed from above, resemble an eagle with its wings spread.

You know better! The town abuts that portion of Michigan that looks like it *should* belong to Wisconsin. What the hell else is there to do up there but Spread Eagle and get freaky? Hell, even Albert Einstein apparently liked a Spread Eagle vacation, and *he* was a freaking *genius*. Seriously, he knew some folks in Spread Eagle and visited them from time to time.

In addition to Spread Eagle ladies, you also will find scores of Spread Eagle bears, coyote, and deer at the nearby Spread Eagle Barrens State Natural Area. ↗

WHERE IS SPREAD EAGLE?

It's not far from Iron Mountain, just across the border from the Upper Peninsula of Michigan.

WHY IS IT NAMED AFTER THE MISSIONARY POSITION?

In fact, the town is named for a chain of lakes that resemble a spread eagle if viewed from overhead.

WHAT DO YOU NEED TO KNOW ABOUT SPREAD EAGLE?

Einstein enjoyed a Spread Eagle vacation as much as the next hot-blooded guy.

SWASTIKA,
ONTARIO

Each day, apple-cheeked Aryan youngsters in a small corner of Ontario begin school with the words, "I pledge allegiance, to *der fuhrer*." Then, they spend the rest of the afternoon in various team-building exercises: taunting Jewish kids, spreading hate, working toward final solutions. Ah, it's just another fine day in Swastika!

The town was named in 1908 after the local Swastika Gold Mine, so they claimed the name and symbol long before Hitler. And, *boy,* were those Swastikans pissed when World War II came along.

Suddenly, their town was named for a Nazi symbol. The fine folks of the town could have changed the name of their municipality. Local government wanted *Swastika* changed to *Winston* in honor of Churchill.

Swastikans cried, "*Nein!*" Not unlike redneck good ole boys supporting their right to wave the Stars and Bars, locals claimed the name of the town stood for heritage and not hate. Everyone outside of town cried, "Bullshit!" But the name, to this day, sticks.

So, a fine "*Deutschland uber alles*" to you, proud (bone-stupid) Swastikans! ➚

SIEG HEIL! WHERE IS SWASTIKA?

Swastika is in Northern Ontario, near Kirkland Lake.

SIEG HEIL! HOW DID SWASTIKA GET ITS NAME?

The Swastika is a 3,000-year-old symbol that, traditionally, has stood for good luck. So, when some folks decided to start a gold mine in Northern Ontario, they named it for a symbol of good luck. Who knew that Hitler would come along and fuck things up so badly for Swastikans?

SIEG HEIL! WHAT DO YOU NEED TO KNOW ABOUT SWASTIKA?

The town is really, really attached to its name, despite the negative associations all normal people have with swastikas. Community pride is great, but . . . .

TARZAN,
TEXAS

Cities throughout the world have been named for noble figures, but only one town has the nerve to name itself after a fictional character best known for making monosyllabic statements, for beating on his chest, and for making a yell that's damn near impossible to replicate in print, but here goes anyway:
AAAHAHAHAHAAAHAAAHAHAHAHAAAH!

Tarzan, Texas, was *not* named for someone who happened to have the name Tarzan. It's not the Anglicized form of a Native American word. It's not some Spanish term that translates as, say, "place that sucks and that is in the middle of freaking nowhere." Nope. *Tarzan* actually is named for the fictional character created by Edgar Rice Burroughs and popularized on film by Johnny Weissmuller.

Perhaps Tant Lindsay, the man who built the town's first business, was on drugs when he named his fledgling town after Tarzan. After all, it was Lindsay who sent, in 1927, a list of possible names to postal officials. Wasn't that the era when "reefer madness" took hold in the country?

Picture Mr. Lindsay, toking on some of that sticky green, and coming up with prospective names. Perhaps the rest of the names were so fucked-up that those postal officials felt *Tarzan* was the least repulsive. Whatever substances Lindsay was or was not smoking, he named his new town Tarzan, and Tarzan it remains. ↗

WHERE IS TARZAN?
Deep in the heart of Texas.

WHY IS IT NAMED TARZAN?
The town's founder must have been a fan of the Edgar Rice Burroughs character.

WHAT DO YOU NEED TO KNOW ABOUT TARZAN?
Me Tarzan. You Jane.

TAUMATAWHAKATANGIHANGA-KOAUAUOTAMATEAPOKAIWHEN-UAKITANATAHU HILL,

NEW ZEALAND

"Holy shit that's a long goddamn name" is the rough translation of the above 1,000-foot hill, which is found in New Zealand's Hawke's Bay region. The region is known for its internationally famous wines, and overindulgence might explain the name, Taumatawhakatangihangakoauauotamateapokaiwhenuakitanatahu, which is one of the world's longest.

In fact, Taumatawhakatangihangakoauauotamateapokaiwhenuakitanatahu, comes from the Maori (a local indigenous people), and translated it means, "Takes you longer to say than it does to climb, assmunch."

In truth, the translation is still pretty fucking weird, as it celebrates a god with impressive knees and a pretty bizarre way of trying to get laid (don't try this at home!): "The summit where Tamatea, the man with the big knees, the climber of mountains, the land-swallower who travelled about, played his nose flute to his loved one."

Other versions of the hill's name also include a random mention of Tamatea's circumcised penis. Is it any wonder locals just call the hill Taumata? ⏎

WHERE IS TAUMATAW . . . OH, FUCK IT. WHERE IS THIS THING?

The 1,000-foot hill is in the Hawke's Bay region of New Zealand, where people spend most of their lives learning how to pronounce correctly the name of the goddamn hill.

WHY DOES THE HILL HAVE THIS RIDICULOUSLY LONG GODDAMN NAME?

It's Maori. It celebrates indigenous culture. Stop being so closed to other traditions, asshole.

WHAT DO YOU NEED TO KNOW ABOUT THIS HILL?

It's got a very long name.

TE PUKE,
NEW ZEALAND

Vomit and citrus make strange, and pretty damn icky, bedfellows in this New Zealand town.

Te Puke means "the hill" in Maori and should be pronounced "teh-pook-eh," rather than like the stuff you leave all over the back of your buddy's car. The delightful, non-vomit-inducing climate of Te Puke makes it a great spot for growing lemons and oranges. The town bills itself as "The Kiwifruit Capital of the World."

While in Te Puke, be sure to visit Kiwi360. At this theme park, you can ride in a kiwicart underneath the world's largest kiwifruit whilst sipping on a fresh glass of kiwifruit juice before buying kiwifruit-shaped jewelry. Yep . . . enough kiwi-themed garbage for you Te Puke up yer guts. See you there! ↗

WHERE CAN I GO TE PUKE?

In New Zealand's Bay of Plenty region, where you can party 'til yeh puke.

WHY DOES THIS NAME MAKE ME WANT TE PUKE?

Early New Zealand settlers called the Maori were not expressing disgust with the area. They named it after its many hills.

WHAT DO I NEED TO KNOW IN ORDER TE PUKE?

If, like many, kiwifruit makes you want to barf, upchuck, blow chunks, disgorge, yak, or call Earl on the porcelain phone, then you'll know to avoid Te Puke, "The Kiwifruit Capital of the World."

TIGHTSQUEEZE,
VIRGINIA

Virginia used to claim it was "for lovers," even though there is no reason to believe that people there score more often than the rest of us. Perhaps the people disappointed in the lack of follow through on the state motto were busy finding hookers or lobbyists—same thing—on the streets of Washington, D.C. and Northern Virginia. If they go south to Pittsylvania County, however, there is a community called *Tightsqueeze*. Surely, in a place like that, anyone can get lucky.

Tightsqueeze earned its name because of a couple of businesses. A main thoroughfare went through town, and a local merchant, W.H. Colbert, built his general store very close to the road so that women travelers could go straight from their carriages and into his shop without touching the often-muddy ground. Before long, a blacksmith built *his* shop, right up against the road, directly across from Colbert's store. The resulting tight squeeze forced travelers to slow down as they passed through town.

Now, you would think folks in a town named *Tightsqueeze* would be embarrassed by such a patently stupid name. You would imagine that they would pause before answering the simple, harmless question: Where do you live?

Well, you would be *wrong*. Not long ago, Pittsylvania County leaders attempted to change the name of the unincorporated community to "Fairview." Now, *that* is a pretty—and completely *not* funny—name. Tightsqueezers went batshit. The name remains. ↗

> **WHERE IS TIGHTSQUEEZE?**
>
> Tightsqueeze is in Southern Virginia's Pittsylvania County.
>
> **WHY IS IT CALLED *TIGHTSQUEEZE*?**
>
> Once upon a time, two businesses that faced each other were so close to the road that they caused travelers a tight squeeze on the way through town.
>
> **WHAT DO YOU NEED TO KNOW ABOUT TIGHTSQUEEZE?**
>
> Nah. You wouldn't get lucky *there*, either.

TIGHTWAD,
MISSOURI

Finally, the perfect spot for cheapos has been found, right smack dab in the in the middle (well, a little to the west of the exact middle, but you get the idea) of Missouri.

In Tightwad, no one gets a free ride. Shit no! Lost your job? Tough shit. Things are tough all over. Now, pay up!

Dang, life is *tough* in Tightwad. These folks are *serious*.

After all, rumor has it that the town's name derives from an incident involving a miserly grocer. Not content to get a fair price for a watermelon (some say a rooster), the grocer forced a customer to pay fifty cents more for the pick of the watermelon/rooster litter.

Uh oh, bad choice. The customer was a postal worker. Before postal workers wielded power by, well, *going postal*, they wielded power by having a great say in the naming of communities. This particular postman got royally pissed, and Tightwad, Missouri, was born.

Nowadays, the people of Tightwad pinch their pennies until every bit of copper is extracted from the zinc. Then, they sit and lord it over anyone who is less fortunate. And, chances are, the local grocers still screw over people who love watermelons (and roosters). ↗

PLEASE, SIR, MAY I HAVE SOME MORE?

No! This is Tightwad, Missouri, in Henry County.

WHY ARE YOU SUCH A TIGHTWAD?

Supposedly, the name *Tightwad* arose when an angry postal worker was cheated by a parsimonious shop keeper.

BUDDY, CAN YOU SPARE A DIME?

Get the fuck out of here.

TITZ,
GERMANY

Dang, look at those things. They're freakin' *huge*! I'd like to climb all over them. Yep, there's nothing like Germany's Alps. If you're looking for Titz, ironically, it's a community that's nowhere near the mountains. It's only a few hundred feet above sea level. But, surely, with a name like that, the local *frauleins* are well-endowed, so you really should visit Titz.

A not-unheard-of German surname, *Titz* is most likely named for a family that settled in the area back when a swastika was simply an ancient symbol for good luck. Titz is good-sized, at some three hundred square miles, and the community holds about 9,000 Titzites? Titzlers? Titties? Whatever funny thing the people there are called.

Finally, even though Titz is flat, the district of Duren in which one can find Titz, does include portions of the Eifel hills. Perhaps you can see Titz from there, if you're looking for Titz. But if you really want to feel the Titz experience, you should grab some sturdy shoes and amble all over Titz. ↗

WHERE IS TITZ?

On 50 percent of the world's population. Oh, and in Germany's Duren district.

WHY IS THIS PLACE NAMED *TITZ*?

Apparently, it was named for a family with that name who once settled in the community.

WHAT DO YOU NEED TO KNOW ABOUT TITZ?

They have very sensitive nipples.

TOAD SUCK,
ARKANSAS

Admit it. You've been horny enough to do some strange things . . . and people, for that matter. You woke up the next day, feeling like shit, staring at the form in the bed next to you, and you shuddered, wondering how the hell you could extract yourself from such an unpleasant situation. We've all been there.

But, bestiality? Surely not. Cored apples, maybe. But animals? And especially . . . toads? Sure, we've heard of horny toads, but . . . get real.

In truth, *Toad Suck* got its colorful name from the card sharks and riverboat men who wound up in this small community near Little Rock. The good Christians of the community would say that these men of ill repute "sucked up whiskey like toads," which, semantically, makes no sense.

Toads don't drink whiskey, and most normal people don't suck up toads. But you wouldn't know anything about normal, so why argue? Another possibility for the name is that a *suck*, like a *lick*, is the name given to natural salt deposits that attract animals.

Nowadays, Toad Suck lacks gamblers, but it does have the annual Toad Suck Daze, which offers a range of activities designed to raise funds for area schools. The fun includes music, crafts, toad races, and a circle jerk involving toads of all shapes and sizes. ⤴

WHERE IS TOAD SUCK?

Wherever really horny men encounter really horny toads.

WHY IS IT NAMED AFTER SUCKING TOADS?

Supposedly, folks in the area said that the inveterate gamblers and riverboat men who gathered at this community near the Arkansas River "sucked up whiskey like toads."

WHAT DO YOU NEED TO KNOW ABOUT TOAD SUCK?

Toad Suck Daze doesn't really have any toad-involving circle jerk competitions . . . at least so far as we know.

TOM, DICK, AND HARRY MOUNTAIN,

OREGON

Believe it or not, it took a while for this three-peaked mountain to gain its generic name. Some folks were calling it Tom, Dick, and Harry Mountain as far back as the turn of the previous century, but for some reason, the peaks came to be called *Tom Dick Mountain*.

Perhaps, stupid people thought the mountain was named for a guy named *Tom Dick*. They didn't make the connection that the two-mile-long mountain in Oregon's Clackamas County had *three* distinct peaks at its summit.

For generations the Tom Dick/Tom, Dick, and Harry debate raged. Finally, in 1969, the United States Board on Geographic Names finally agreed that they were just wild about Harry, and he was added to the mountain's name.

Nowadays, Tom, Dick, and Harry is home to the Mount Hood Skibowl ski resort. Women from throughout the country come out to ski its slopes and look for someone to take back to their lodge rooms. But don't get overconfident . . . wait for it . . . wait for it . . . they won't go to bed with just any Tom, Dick, and Harry. ↗

HOW TALL IS TOM, DICK, AND HARRY?

It's just under a mile in height and two miles in length.

WHY IS IT NAMED TOM, DICK, AND HARRY?

For a while, it was just Tom Dick Mountain. Then, around 1969, *Harry* was added. The name apparently came about as a result of the mountain being, well, just another mountain.

WHAT DO YOU NEED TO KNOW ABOUT TOM, DICK, AND HARRY MOUNTAIN?

It is home to a popular ski resort.

TOMBSTONE,
ARIZONA

Just because you've probably heard of Tombstone, Arizona doesn't make the name any less fucked up. Calling a place you hope will attract people *Tombstone* is like naming a fast food restaurant *E. coli*.

Tombstone is best known for being the location of the infamous OK Corral and for having the quintessential Boot Hill Cemetery, so named because more folks in the early, prospecting days of the community died with their boots on—i.e., by misadventure or murder—than from natural causes.

Town founder Ed Schieffelin first arrived in the area to stake a mining claim. After he filed his claim, Schieffelin named it *Tombstone*. Why? Schieffelin was bragging about his claim to a passing soldier who told him that the only rock he would be likely to uncover in a waterless shithole subject to Apache attacks was a tombstone. Instead, Schieffelin found a huge vein of silver. He named the boomtown that grew up around his mine after the original claim, as a sort-of "fuck you" to the soldier who'd suggested it in the first place.

In its heyday, Tombstone was a town of 1,500 residents and featured many back-east amenities, such as ice skating. By 1900, much of the town had burned down, the silver was pretty much gone, and folks realized they were living in the middle of the fucking desert. Tombstone did not write its epitaph, however. The town was its county seat, and by the middle of the twentieth century, all that "shootout at the OK Corral" and "Boot Hill" bullshit was tourist gold. ↗

WHERE IS TOMBSTONE?

Tombstone is the county seat of Cochise County, which borders Mexico.

WHY IS IT NAMED FOR A TOMBSTONE?

The guy who founded the town was a miner. When the miner bragged about his new claim, some wiseass told him that the only rock he'd ever mine in the area would be a tombstone. The miner found silver, struck it rich, and named his town *Tombstone*.

WHAT DO YOU NEED TO KNOW ABOUT TOMBSTONE?

It has a newspaper called the *Tombstone Epitaph*. It draws tourists eager for a taste of the authentic Old West.

TRIM,
IRELAND

Everyone wants some trim, right? Ask any guy—from Tiger Woods to Bill Clinton—and he'll tell you that trim is impossible to resist. In Ireland, you'll find the tidiest Trim in all the world. It's official! Ireland's Trim has been named the tidiest *twice*. Who, after all, wants sloppy trim . . . unless beer goggles are involved.

Trim, Ireland is in County Meath. It's not just got Trim; it's got the largest Trim in Western Europe. It's true! Trim is home to Castle Trim. There's so much Trim there that Mel Gibson visited during the filming of *Braveheart*! Hey, if it's good enough for Mel . . . .

Other than as a nod to the town's delightful young lasses, Trim's name comes from the Gaelic phrase: *baile atha troim*. Translated, the words mean "best beaver in Western Europe" or, possibly, "town at the ford of elderflowers."

The quality of Ireland's Trim isn't just recognized on Earth. Recently, Trim has become a hotbed of UFO activity. What appeared to be a fleet of UFOs was spotted intermittently from 2008 and into 2009, in the skies over the community. Apparently, Ireland's Trim is out of this world! ➚

WHERE IS TRIM?

Ireland's County Meath.

WHY IS IT NAMED AFTER PUDENDA?

The name derives from a Gaelic phrase that means "town at the ford of elderflowers."

WHAT DO YOU NEED TO KNOW ABOUT TRIM?

Lots, because you're never gonna get any, bruh.

TRUTH OR CONSEQUENCES,
NEW MEXICO

It's a well-known fact that most folks would sell out their mothers—even their grandmothers—for a chance at fame. But who would be willing to sell out an entire town? The good folks of Hot Springs, New Mexico, of course.

Hot Springs was named for local hot springs that brought spa enthusiasts to this town, a couple hundred miles south of Albuquerque. All that changed in 1950.

Ralph Edwards, host of a now-pretty-much-forgotten-but-once-really-really-popular radio quiz show called *Truth or Consequences*, announced he would air the show from any town willing to change its name to, well, Truth or Consequences. Municipal greed kicked in, and Hot Springs was no more.

To this day, Truth or Consequences is proud of its game show origins, holding all sorts of fiestas and pageantry to commemorate the transmission of that game show from within its corporate limits. Like Happy, Texas (see page 94), Hollywood producers thought the town's name was so cool that they borrowed it for a film's title . . . a film of which not a single frame was shot in Truth or Consequences, New Mexico. ↗

> **WHAT'S THE TRUTH?**
> Truth or Consequences is the seat of New Mexico's Sierra County.

> **WHAT ARE THE CONSEQUENCES?**
> *Hot Springs*, a name that had served perfectly well for years, was changed to honor a game show, in hopes of drawing attention and tourist dollars.

> **IS THAT YOUR FINAL ANSWER?**
> There is no truth to the rumor that Truth or Consequences is considering a name change to Dancing with the Stars, New Mexico.

TURDA,
ROMANIA

A city defeated by Rome, in order to gain access to its salt mines. An early Saxon stronghold. Site of a meeting that allowed Roman Catholics and early Lutherans to co-exist peacefully. Yet, to most English speakers, Turda, Romania, is just a city that seems to be named after shit.

In fact, *Turda* is named for Thor, he of the large hammer and thunder, old Marvel comics, and Thursday (yep, named for Thor). He may have been a Nordic god, but nature must have called him as well. And when he let go, surely the sound of Thor's turdas must have rattled like thunder through the forests.

Turda's salt mines were around long before recorded history, and they led Rome to conquer the area and turn it into a *colonia*, or major city. The mines closed in the 1930s but were used as shelters from German bombs during World War II.

Yes, Turda has had an important place in the world's history, yet it continues to be best known as a place named after poop. Way to go, Turda! ↗

I'VE GOT TO GO . . . NOW.

Turda can be found along the banks of the Aries River. You probably shouldn't swim in it.

WHERE'S THE BEST PLACE TO DROP A DEUCE?

Turda, of course. It was named in honor of Thor.

WHAT A LOAD . . .

Turda's salt mines have become a big tourist draw.

TWATT,
SCOTLAND

For Americans, *twat* is a vulgar word for the vagina. For most Brits, *twat* brings to mind an insulting word for a person one finds stupid, contemptible, and idiotic. It's equivalent to the American insult, *douchebag*. But for some Scots, *twat* just sounds like home.

Twatt is a delightful, small community found on Scotland's Shetland Islands. The name is a modernization of an Old Norse word meaning "small parcel of land." Or it might be an Old Norse word meaning "douchebag." Either way, to modern ears, the village's name is salacious, insulting, or both.

Since the 1970s, the Shetland Islands' population has grown due to the discovery of oil and gas found just offshore. Either that, or it has grown because so many men are attracted to the beauty of Twatt. ↗

WHERE IS TWATT?

(Giggle.) Oh, sorry. It's to be found among Scotland's Shetland Islands.

HOW DID IT GET THE NAME *TWATT*?

The name is a modernized form of Old Norse word meaning "small parcel of land" or, perhaps, an Old Norse word meaning "douchebag."

WHAT DO I NEED TO KNOW ABOUT TWATT?

(Still giggling . . .) Oh, sorry. Waters off the Shetland Islands have been a drilling site for oil and gas since the 1970s.

TWO EGG,
FLORIDA

Two Egg is in the part of Florida that most Floridians would happily cede to southern Alabama or to southern Georgia. It's not the site of tasty babes and tasty waves, beautiful sunsets, and tons of tourist dollars. Nope. It's the part of the upper panhandle that serves as a reminder of what "dirt poor" looks like.

That, in fact, is how this oddly named community got its name. Two Egg was settled around the time of the Civil War and first had the name *Allison*, after a family that built early businesses in the community. *Allison*. Not a bad name. Kind of pretty.

Then came the Great Depression. Jobs dried up. Families starved. The town, like many others, was devastated. A local store, owned by John Henry Pittman, remained. He began to trade goods for eggs. Eventually, folks came to calling his place the *two egg store*. The name stuck.

Two Egg remains a place where you won't find a whole lot of prosperity nor a chicken in every pot. Most of the town's businesses have closed. In fact, the town is now best known for its weird name and for its ghost. A bride, who appears to be on fire, is said to haunt a local bridge.

You know what? This place is depressing. Screw it. Head south to Palm Beach and try to get lucky or head to Miami to dirty dance with a guy who looks suspiciously like Don Johnson. Stay away from Two Egg unless you just want to get bummed out. ↗

WHERE IS TWO EGG?

Two Egg is in Jackson County, Florida, which borders both Georgia and Alabama.

WHY IS IT NAMED *TWO EGG*?

A storekeeper helped keep people from starving during the Great Depression by trading goods for eggs.

WHAT DO YOU NEED TO KNOW ABOUT TWO EGG?

It's depressing as shit.

UGLEY,
ENGLAND

Just because Brits have substandard dental work, fish-belly-white skin, and smell of Bass Ale doesn't mean they're all ugly. England has given birth to models, actors, and actresses, all of whom prove that there are some beautiful people in the Mother Country.

But most folks around the world—shit, even most Englanders—would probably concede that their country has more than its fair share of ugly. Oh, and Brits can't spell either. They're always adding "u's" to words like *colour* or *valour*. They add extra consonants and vowels to words like *shoppe*.

Combine the ugliness of Brits with their notorious inability to spell words properly, and you've got the tiny hamlet of Ugley. Once known as *Butt Ugley*, the town has, for centuries, just been *Ugley*.

Picture all the Ugley folks riding their Ugley bicycles and shopping for Ugley groceries at Ugley supermarkets. Do visitors to town spend most of their time vomiting from all the disgusting Ugleyness? Do residents sometimes wear paper bags on their heads in order not to frighten non-Ugley children?

Ugley's original name was not *Butt Ugley*. In fact, it was *Uggele*. Then, it became *Ugghelea*. Finally, it became just plain *Ugley*. The name most likely means something along the lines of "woodland clearing of a man named Ugga."

So, one man's ugly name has led to an Ugley community. If you visit, you'll find Ugley folks are quite pleasant. They're just Butt Ugley, that's all. ➷

WHERE IS UGLEY?
It's in your mirror.

WHY IS IT NAMED UGLEY?
Most likely, the town's name goes *way* back in history and refers to the land of a man named Ugga.

WHAT DO YOU NEED TO KNOW ABOUT UGLEY?
It has a funny name.

UNALASKA,
ALASKA

Okay, here's a quick lesson in etymology. We'll keep it simple in case you're not very bright. If one puts the prefix *un* before something, you are suggesting it is *not* like the root word that follows.

For example, idiotic wing nuts tend to call anyone who does not believe in their narrow-minded ideology *un-American.* This is supposed to suggest that people who do not believe in X are *not* American. If you are *un*interested, then you are *not* interested. If you are *un*usual, then you are *not* usual.

So, what does one make of *Un*alaska, Alaska? It certainly *looks* like Alaska. It has pristine lakes, snow-covered mountains, active volcanoes, and it's as cold as shit. Unalaska is pretty far west among the Aleutian Islands, so this may be one of those places Sarah Palin could stand in order to see Russia.

Nonetheless, the town's name suggests that the community is, most emphatically, *not* Alaska. That's pretty freaking weird. How did this happen? Blame the natives.

Aleuts or Unangans have lived in the area for thousands of years. They called their land *Ounalashka,* which means "near the peninsula." After white folks came to the area and claimed it for their own, they changed the name slightly to *Unalaska.* So, on second thought, don't blame the natives. Blame the white people. ✈

WHERE IS UNALASKA?

It is located on Unalaska Island. Duh!

WHY IS IT NAMED UNALASKA?

Native Alaskans called the island *Ounalaska,* which means "near the peninsula." White people came along and changed the name to the oxymoronic *Unalaska.*

WHAT DO YOU NEED TO KNOW ABOUT UNALASKA?

It is one of the rainiest places in the United States. It rains 250 days a year in Unalaska.

VULCAN,
CANADA

Since it first appeared on television nearly forty years ago, *Star Trek*—the series and the later series and the movie and the later movies and all the merchandising—has possessed the consciousness of a certain kind of person. That person is called by many names: *dweeb, dork, geek, loser*, etc. One portion of these losers has adopted the name *Trekkie* because of a shared love of the show/movie/fountain of merchandising bullshit. Well, Trekkies of the world unite. We've got just the place for you: Vulcan, Alberta.

Vulcan was named in 1915 by a surveyor for the Canadian Pacific Railway. Of course, unless he'd gone through one of those *Star Trek* time–space continuum warps, then he had no knowledge that, someday, Mr. Spock would come from the planet Vulcan. This railroad surveyor was thinking of the Roman God of Fire, also named Vulcan. For decades, Vulcan capitalized on being named for a classical god. Most of its streets were named after gods and goddesses. By the 1960s, however, the small agricultural town of Vulcan got something of a tourism boon in the form of Mr. Spock's home planet. So, Vulcan said, "Screw the gods!" Vulcanites focused instead on attracting Trekkies. Vulcan has the Tourism and Trek Station, which contains *Star Trek* memorabilia and such. Outside, you can find a model of the Enterprise used in *Star Trek V*.

So, take a trip to Vulcan. While you're there, live long and prosper . . . just don't come back here. Trekkies are irritating. ➚

WHERE IS VULCAN?

Vulcan is in the southern part of Alberta, Canada.

WHY IS IT NAMED AFTER MR. SPOCK'S HOME PLANET?

It's actually named for the Roman God of Fire.

WHAT DO YOU NEED TO KNOW ABOUT VULCAN?

It's filled with *Star Trek* crap.

WALL DRUG,
SOUTH DAKOTA

Free ice water. That's all it took to make a drug store in the middle of nowhere into a tourist attraction known the world over. Shit, there's a Wall Drug sign at the South Pole, for Chrissakes.

In 1931, a Nebraska native named Ted Hustead decided to open a drug store in Wall. Since Wall is a Podunk town on the South Dakota prairie, business was slow. Then, his wife, Dorothy, got the brilliant idea to offer free ice water to anyone willing to stop at Wall Drug.

The first of what would become hundreds, possibly thousands, of Wall Drug billboards and signs sprang up, attracting folks on their way to Mount Rushmore, the only other thing worth visiting in South Dakota.

Nowadays, Wall Drug is a sprawling, western-themed complex that sells all the totally worthless shit that kids and drunk college students can't live without. In addition, Wall Drug boasts a giant dinosaur, continues to offer free ice water, and treats customers to the dulcet sounds of the Wall Drug Cowboy Orchestra, scary-looking mannequins that sing shit-kicking tunes while staring at you with flat, glazed-looking, dilated-pupil eyes.

Not bad for the middle of fucking nowhere! ⬈

WHERE IS WALL DRUG?

In Wall. Duh!

WHO CARES ABOUT WALL DRUG?

The thousands of people who visit the place and then put up signs indicating the distance to Wall Drug. Also, it's just a weird, surreal place that shouldn't, by all rights, exist.

WHAT DO YOU NEED TO KNOW ABOUT WALL DRUG?

It offers free ice water and sells cups of coffee for a nickel.

WANKER'S CORNER,
OREGON

Although the term isn't as common in the States, most Americans know that Brits call the act of masturbation *wanking* and that a *wanker* is not just one who masturbates frequently but, by extension, is a total dweeb who can't get any to save his life. Come to think of it . . . he's a lot like you.

So, how did a town full of Wankers come to find itself situated in Oregon? Well, folks in the community pronounce the name "wahn-ker," for one thing, and the only sizeable business in this unincorporated township is Wanker's Country Store. The community is named for the Wankers who founded the store and settled in the area.

Not far from the country store is the Wanker's Corner Saloon and Café, which is well aware of the double entendre included in its name. For many years, the business sold T-shirts featuring a drawing of a kangaroo eating peanuts from its pouch. The slogan? "Grab your nuts in Wanker's Corner."

Many a passing Brit or Irishman has made a special trip to the saloon just to get a picture of himself proudly proclaiming himself an official Wanker. ↗

WHERE IS IT, YOU WANKER?

Wanker's Corner is in Clackamas County, Oregon, not far from the Washington border.

WHY IS IT NAMED AFTER PEOPLE WHO LIKE TO MASTURBATE?

It isn't, really. It's named for the family who started the Wanker's Country Store in the area.

COME OFF IT, YOU WANKER.

Fun-lovin' Anglos like to visit the town just to get a picture in front of the Wanker's Corner Saloon and Café, about five miles from the original country store.

WEE WAA,
AUSTRALIA

The so-called Cotton Capital of Australia is in a town that sounds like something an infant would say.

First off, who the hell even knew Australia *has* cotton? Isn't that just found in the southeastern United States in places that used to practice slavery and that now just practice unrestrained racism?

No! It turns out that Wee Waa, in Australia's New South Wales, grows a lot of cotton ($140 million worth) and has giant levees built around it . . . just like Louisiana! In addition, the town has a funny-sounding name. What more could the fine citizens of Wee Waa want out of life?

Well, the town also has a problem with dark-skinned people . . . just like Louisiana! In 1981, an aboriginal man was killed while in custody in a Wee Waa police station. The death prompted a massive investigation.

Perhaps *that's* why the town has the name *Wee Waa*. The words mean "fire for roasting" in the local aboriginal dialect. Once the authorities got "burned" for their naughtiness, they were "roasted" like weenies over a campfire!

Today, Wee Waa is a place in which, as Rodney King wished, everyone can just get along. ↗

> **WHERE IS WEE WAA?**
>
> Wee Waa is in the Australian state of New South Wales, which is Australia's most populous state.

> **WHY IS IT NAMED WEE WAA?**
>
> In the local aboriginal language, the words mean "fire for roasting." Why the town is called "fire for roasting" is unclear.

> **WHAT DO YOU NEED TO KNOW ABOUT WEE WAA?**
>
> It's the cotton capital of Australia!

WEED,
CALIFORNIA

Dang, now wouldn't you *know* that a town named for marijuana would be found in California? It's not even funny to learn this because . . . where the fuck *else* would you find a city named *Weed*?

Now that "medicinal marijuana clinics" are sprouting up like, well, weeds all over Los Angeles, a state already known as a pot-smoker's paradise, it has become nirvana, paradise, heaven, and that place with all the virgins that Muslim extremists go rolled into one. Long before weed could be found on more street corners than Starbucks, however, there was one community proud to let its pot flag fly.

Weed is in Siskiyou County. What, you know the way to San Jose but not to Siskiyou? Well, neither did we. Turns out it's up at the Oregon border and once was a hotbed of Gold Rush fever. Apparently, once the gold dried up, the town turned to other means of staying afloat. Siskiyou let San Francisco have a lock on opium dens, and it opted for Weed.

What? Oh, bummer, dude. Turns out that Weed is named for town founder, Abner Weed. Of course, for all we know, he was such a pothead that he's the man who lent his name to one of marijuana's many nicknames. Even if that's not the case, Weed is still supposed to be a beautiful place.

So, score some down in L.A. for medicinal purposes, then take your weed up to Weed and enjoy the Cascade Mountains. Just make sure you pick up plenty of munchies before your journey north. ↗

WHERE IS WEED?

Weed is in Siskiyou County, near the Oregon border.

WHY IS IT NAMED AFTER MARIJUANA?

Weed was named for town founder, Abner Weed.

WHAT DO YOU NEED TO KNOW ABOUT WEED?

It should be legalized, man!

WET BEAVER WILDERNESS,
ARIZONA

Someone either was a fucking idiot or a freaking genius when he—and it *must* have been a he—found a delightful creek about fifty miles away from Flagstaff and named it for the creatures he found gallivanting there. The result is Wet Beaver Creek.

Just think about it . . . you've been hiking for miles. You're tired. You're hungry. But most of all, you're horny. And then, there it is: acres of wet beaver! Talk about Valhalla!

The creek has given its name to a wilderness area in Arizona's Coconino National Forest. Among the delights to be found in the Wet Beaver Wilderness are hiking trails, fishing spots, camping sites, and, of course, plenty of wet beaver.

Portions of the Wet Beaver Wilderness are difficult to find, but you know how men are . . . they'll crawl across broken glass or swim in a cesspool for some of that wet beaver. Wet Beaver is hard to find, but it's worth the trip. ↗

> **WHERE IS WET BEAVER WILDERNESS?**
>
> It's part of the Coconino National Forest, not far from Sedona, Arizona.

> **WHY IS IT NAMED *WET BEAVER*?**
>
> Unfortunately, for horny guys everywhere, it's simply named for the dam-building animal.

> **WHAT DO YOU NEED TO KNOW ABOUT WET BEAVER?**
>
> Snicker. Snicker.

WETWANG,
ENGLAND

If you're one of those um, cool dudes who treat *The Lord of the Rings* like it's some sort of holy scripture, then you may associate this Yorkshire community with Middle Earth. Otherwise, the village will bring to mind a post-coital penis.

Most likely, Wetwang owes its name to the Old Norse language. Possibly, the name translates to "field set aside for trials." Perhaps it means "wet field." Or perchance it means "Sorry, baby, it's your turn to lie in the wet spot."

Wetwang is known to some for its black swans and for a chariot cemetery left over from the Iron Age. While, for others, the village is known for bringing to mind a post-coital penis. Those silly, slapstick-lovin' Brits have laughed their arses off over Wetwang for generations. ↗

WHERE CAN I WET MY WANG?

Wetwang is a community of about 700 people in England's Yorkshire region. Apparently, people there have sex a lot.

WHY IS NAMED AFTER A POST-COITAL PENIS?

Well, it's actually connected to the Old Norse word *vangr*, which means "field."

WHAT DO YOU NEED TO KNOW ABOUT WETWANG?

Even most Brits find the name funny.

WHAT CHEER,
IOWA

Sure, there's not much going on in Iowa. A movie back in the 1980s tried to suggest that Iowa was tantamount to heaven, but that's really only true insofar as Iowa is a place you'd have to be dead to enjoy. Nonetheless, it is startling that one of the state's communities seems to point out the *ennui* of day-to-day Iowan life: What Cheer.

Indeed! What Cheer? Where is it? Will you find it amid the acres of grain and whatever the hell else it is that folks grow in Iowa? Will you find it on wind-swept prairies home only to gophers? Will you find it in the middle of nowhere, which is the location of pretty much the entire state?

Maybe. But you certainly will *not* find it in a small, Keokuk County town. What Cheer is the English translation of a greeting Native Americans used with Puritan settlers in New England. Over time, the words became a popular toast.

That *still* doesn't really explain why a town in the Midwest pays homage to a greeting from seventeenth-century New England. Of course, Shakespeare used the greeting in one of his last works, *The Tempest*, but does anyone really believe that Iowans are paying homage to the Bard? That would require them to have the ability to read. ↗

WHERE IS WHAT CHEER?

It's in Keokuk County, which makes it not the middle of nowhere, but nowhere itself.

WHY IS IT CALLED *WHAT CHEER*?

Because, clearly, there is no cheer to be found in this nowhere town.

WHAT DO YOU NEED TO KNOW ABOUT WHAT CHEER?

Not a damn thing.

WHOREHOUSE MEADOW,
OREGON

Ah, the Old West. The id was king! Everyone was out to get rich quick, kill anyone who got in the way, and bust a nut with anything wearing a skirt . . . including any skirt-wearing antelope that might have wandered into camp.

One spot, in Oregon's Harney County, was home to a popular whorehouse. Horny prospectors, fishermen, and settlers conquered, saw, and came repeatedly in the temporary buildings that housed the red light district near Fish Lake.

Even though the prostitutes are long gone (only to be found on craigslist.com), Whorehouse Meadow remains. But it almost disappeared. The nation's Bureau of Land Management (the same folks who fucked over Indians for generations) decided that *Whorehouse Meadow* was inappropriate.

The BLM changed the name on official maps to "Naughty Girl Meadows." Folks in Oregon went apeshit. How *dare* the federal government remove our state's whorehouse? How could they possibly remove this piece of our state's culture and heritage? That sort of thing.

When the legal dust settled in 1981, Whorehouse Meadow was back, apparently to stay. God bless free enterprise and open-minded states! ↗

WHERE IS WHOREHOUSE MEADOW?

It's on the west slope of Oregon's Steens Mountain, which is near Frenchglen.

WHY IS IT NAMED *WHOREHOUSE MEADOW*?

Because whorehouses used to operate there. Duh!

WHAT DO YOU NEED TO KNOW ABOUT WHOREHOUSE MEADOWS?

Some maps identify the area as Whorehouse Meadows, plural.

WHY,
ARIZONA

Well, why the fuck *not* Arizona? I mean, it's a nice enough state. It's got mountains and those giant cacti and a couple of large cities. It's not far from Las Vegas, if the gambling bug bites you. Of course, this particular community is much closer to Mexico than it is to Vegas, but—that said—it's also pretty close to the mondo-cool Organ Pipe Cactus National Monument.

So, overall, Arizona's not bad. Why, then, does the state that brought you Nothing (see page 149) also bring you Why?

Well, if the folks of Why had had their druthers, the town actually would be named Y. The community gets its name from the one-time intersection of State Highways 85 and 86. Once upon a time, these highways met in a "Y" shape.

Apparently, state law at the time demanded that any new community have at least three letters in its name. So, the "powers that be" settled on Why. The irony is that, since the town was developed, the Y-intersection has been replaced and no longer exists.

So, there is no good answer to the question: Why is Why *Why*? It is what it is. ↗

> ### WHERE IS WHY?
> Why is just north of the Mexican border in Arizona's Pima County.

> ### WHY IS IT *WHY*?
> The town is named for a Y-shaped intersection that once existed in town. State law required the community have at least three letters.

> ### WHAT DO YOU NEED TO KNOW ABOUT WHY?
> Why do you care?

WHYNOT,
NORTH CAROLINA

There's indecisive, and then there's *indecisive*. If you can't decide between the navy blue and the gray blazer, then you're merely indecisive. If you're annoying the waiter by floundering between fish and fowl, then that's just indecisive. If you throw up your hands and just say "Fuck it!" and the result is that your town's name is Whynot, then, you're *indecisive*.

Whynot is an unincorporated town in North Carolina's Randolph County. As you drive up to this (barely) wide spot in the road, you see a friendly sign that states, "You are now entering Whynot, North Carolina." At first, you may suspect a prankster is messing about with you. But no! The sign is genuine. And it's a good example of why the saying, "You get what you deserve," exists.

Way back when, folks in this little pissant burg were trying to figure out what to name their town. The conversations began to get heated. You can imagine. One guy wants to name the community after his mother, but for another guy, *Mabel* is the name of that bitch who left him with four hungry children and a crop in the field. So it goes.

Finally, the folks just got sick of arguing over "why not" this and "why not" that and decided just to call the place *Whynot.* A few suggested *Why the Hell Not,* but that was struck down because it might anger God, and God is extremely important in Randolph County, North Carolina.

The result? Whynot. The response? Whocares. ↗

WHYNOT?

Whynot is an unincorporated community in North Carolina's mostly rural Randolph County.

NO, REALLY. WHYNOT?

Well, because no one could come up with anything better. Folks got tired of arguing about their new community's name, threw up their hands, shouted "Fuck it!" and allowed their town to be called Whynot.

FOR REAL, WHYNOT?

Whynot might be the perfect place for you if you're a big fan of ambivalence.

WINCHESTER MYSTERY HOUSE,
CALIFORNIA

The largest, weirdest house in the United States was built to satisfy the whims of ghosts. No shit. It's true. Those ghosts must have been dropping some killer acid because the house has hundreds of rooms, staircases that lead nowhere, and doors that open onto walls. Here's how it all went down.

Oliver Winchester invented the repeating rifle, and it was the gun used to kills Injuns during the time Americans decided the land belonged to *them*, goddammit. Winchester made a fortune. He married a woman named Sarah, had a daughter . . . all was delightful (as long as you weren't no damn Injun).

Then, Oliver Winchester died. So did the couple's daughter. Sarah Winchester went, shall we say, a wee bit batshit. She went to a psychic who told her that the deaths of her loved ones were the result of vengeful spirits killed by the Winchester repeating rifle. And now those spirits were out to kick *her* ass.

The solution? Build a house for the spirits. Keep building that house. In fact, build that house 24/7/365 or else . . . it's curtains for you, lady. Sarah moved to San Jose, bought a small farmhouse and began to turn it into the monstrosity that exists today. ➚

WHERE IS THE WINCHESTER MYSTERY HOUSE?

Do you know the way to San Jose? Then you know the way to the house.

WHY IS IT MYSTERIOUS?

Because it was built based on plans provided by disembodied spirits . . . or provided by an insane old woman. Either way . . . pretty damn mysterious.

WHAT DO YOU NEED TO KNOW ABOUT THE WINCHESTER MYSTERY HOUSE?

It contains about 160 rooms.

WOODY,
CALIFORNIA

Sure, *woody* describes an area covered by dense forest. It also was mentioned frequently in songs by California's own Beach Boys. That particular "woody" was a kind of car with wood paneling on its side, favored by surfers. The younger set will associate *Woody* with a character in *Toy Story*.

But for the rest of us, a *woody* was, is, and forever shall be a synonym for *erection*, as in, "Dude, that hot babe is giving me a woody." This philosophical digression is presented as an introduction to Woody, a town in California. Was the town named for a hard dick? No, it was named for an early pioneer, Dr. Sparrell Walter Woody. But get this! For years, there was a battle over the name. Some wanted to lose their Woody and get a Weringdale instead.

Why? A few years after Woody arrived, the town was formally planned and laid out by a man named Joseph Weringer, who intended for the community to honor *him*. These Californians wanted their Woody, by God! Over time, Woody became permanent, lasting far longer than those four-hour erections warned about on advertisements for Viagra. ↗

WHERE IS WOODY?
Snicker, snicker.

WHY IS IT NAMED AFTER A SYNONYM FOR *HARD ON*?
It's named for an early pioneer whose last name was Woody.

WHAT DO YOU NEED TO KNOW ABOUT WOODY?
It could have been called Weringdale, but locals demanded Woody.

WORMS,
GERMANY

Most people don't like to think about worms. They're slimy, slithery little nematodes. They are associated with death and rot. When they wash up on the sidewalk after a heavy rainstorm, they stink. They're so dumb, they can crawl around after having their heads removed. Worms just don't really have many pleasant associations. About the only people who really like worms are scientists, fishermen, and toddlers looking for a quick snack.

But there are about 85,000 people in Germany who love Worms. In fact, they live in Worms . . . which sounds pretty nasty, if you want to know the truth.

The name *Worms* is Celtic in origin. *Borbetomagus* was the first name given to this town on the Rhine River. It means "settlement in a watery area." Over time, the Celtic word was replaced with a similar Latin word, *vormatia*. Eventually, *Vormatia* became *Worms*.

Worms actually holds an important place in history. It was the site of the Diet of Worms, which worked wonders on waistlines during the Middle Ages. Oh, wait a minute. Turns out that the Diet of Worms was a meeting of a bunch of Catholic leaders who spent most of their time bitching about that upstart, Martin Luther.

Today, Worms is a place that's actually quite beautiful, despite having a name that suggests death, rot, and drunk fishermen with painfully redolent body odor. ↗

WHERE IS WORMS?

Worms is a city of 85,000 people situated along the Rhine River in southwestern Germany.

WHY IS IT NAMED WORMS?

Worms is a weird and unfortunate modernization of a Latin word, *vormatia*.

WHAT DO YOU NEED TO KNOW ABOUT WORMS?

It was the site of the Diet of Worms.

YAAK,
MONTANA

Earth to Montana: There are no yaks in your state. They are found in the Himalayan Mountains—in Central Asia—and not in North America. Sure, some governors of northern states can claim that proximity to Russia practically *makes* them Russian, but you can't see Mongolia from Montana, so *no dice*.

What's that, Montana? Oh . . . well, shit. How were *we* supposed to know that Yaak takes its name from the Yaak River? OR that *yaak* is a Native American word meaning "arrow"? It sounds like vomit or an extremely hirsute horned animal. Well, pull down our pants and call us ginormous.

Yaak is basically a hippie and neo-hippie enclave that is in extreme-northwest Montana. Many folks in town live off the grid, make handicrafts, and eat granola while burning incense and working methodically through the Kama Sutra.

Sure, it's a beautiful place—if you like rugged scenery and few signs of civilization—but it's Hell on Earth for most urbanites and suburbanites. Folks who think tofu should replace Big Macs will enjoy this rural spot.

For the rest of us, we'll just continue to Yaak into the toilet after having five too many or catching the stomach bug. ➚

> ### WHERE IS YAAK?
> Yaak is in the extreme northwest corner of Montana.
>
> ### WHY IS IT NAMED YAAK?
> It's a Native American word meaning "arrow."
>
> ### WHAT DO YOU NEED TO KNOW ABOUT YAAK?
> It's probably gestating the next Unabomber right this very minute!

ZAP,
NORTH DAKOTA

The only riot ever to occur in North Dakota took place in a community with a weird freaking name. More about the riot later . . . for now, let's consider the name *Zap*. It's catchy, all right. It's different too. And it's got some hip cachet via underground comic book artist R. Crumb's Zap Comix.

Zap was named by a railroad company official for a Ukrainian town that is on roughly the same line of latitude. Folks in the region must have felt that *Zaporizhia* was too tongue-tying or just didn't have enough "zip" to it, so the town shortened the Ukrainian village's name to *Zap*.

Now, about that riot . . . it seems that, in 1969, a North Dakota State University student realized he couldn't afford travel to Florida for spring break. So, he created something he called "Zip to Zap: A Grand Festival of Light and Love."

At first, all was well, but then the town ran out of food, the students got drunk off their asses as students are wont to do, and everyone was generally bummed out because this was, after all, the 1960s when college students were required to be pissed off about something.

The kids started a bonfire, things got out of hand, and the governor called in the state militia. The incident didn't result in any deaths or serious injuries, but it did wind up attracting the national news outlets to this small community. Needless to say, the "Zip to Zap" was not repeated. ↗

WHERE IS ZAP?

Zap is in Mercer County, North Dakota, near a tributary of the Knife River.

WHY IS IT CALLED ZAP?

Because locals didn't know how to spell *Zaporizhia*, which is the Ukrainian town for which Zap was named.

WHAT DO YOU NEED TO KNOW ABOUT ZAP?

It was the site of North Dakota's only riot.

ZZYZX,
CALIFORNIA

Miracle cures offered by a shyster with a penchant for do-it-yourself hemorrhoid-removal kits put a place called Zzyzx on the map.

According to town founder Curtis Howe Springer, zzyzx is the last word in the English language. Like his claims that he was a medical doctor and an ordained Methodist minister, Springer appears also to have made up the word.

In fact, Springer was a radio evangelist back in the 1930s. He claimed to be able to work miracle cures for people, if folks would just send him twenty-five bucks—a fortune in those days. Springer took his money and founded a few different healing centers, including one in the Mojave Desert. Zzyzx had a cross-shaped health spa, a sixty-room hotel, a castle, and even an airstrip that he dubbed Zyport. Howe managed to fleece folks on the property from 1944 until 1974, when the U.S. government forced him to leave.

Nowadays, Zzyzx is known mostly for its exit sign along busy Interstate 15, which takes all manner of sinners from Los Angeles to Las Vegas. Oh, and if you'd like a do-it-yourself hemorrhoid-removal kit, just send fifty bucks. You know . . . inflation. That way, even without visiting Zzyzx, you can go back to being the perfect asshole. ↗

WHERE IS ZZYZX?

It's in the middle of the Mojave Desert, not far from Baker, California.

WTF IS ZZYZX?

It doesn't appear to have any meaning. The con artist who created the town named it Zzyzx because con artists are not nice, normal people.

WHAT DO YOU NEED TO KNOW ABOUT ZZYZX?

It's now the site of the Desert Studies Center, which is attached to California State University.

INDEX

-A-

Acock's Green, England, 1
Alabama, 3, 69
Alaska, 62, 70, 81, 184
Amish, 20, 24
Antarctica, 57, 142
Aquinna, Massachusetts, 2
Arab, Alabama, 3
Area 51, 4
Argentina, 139
Arizona, 45, 92, 111, 149, 162, 177, 190, 194
Arkansas, 6, 14, 76, 175
Australia, 39, 42, 104, 106, 143, 188
Austria, 83

-B-

Bacchus, Utah, 5
Bald Knob, Arkansas, 6
Ball, George, 127
Ball, John, 73
Bangkok, Thailand, 7
Bare, England, 8

Barron, William, 75
Bat Cave, North Carolina, 9
Batman, Turkey, 10
Battiest, Oklahoma, 11
Beaver, Oklahoma, 12
Beclean, Romania, 13
Beedeville, Arkansas, 14
Beer, England, 15
Beer Head, 15
Belchertown, Massachusetts, 16
Belgium, 163
Bigadic, Turkey, 19
Big Bone Lick State Park, 17
Big Ugly Creek, West Virginia, 18
Bird, Larry, 82
Bird-in-Hand, Pennsylvania, 20
Bitche, France, 21
Bliss, Idaho, 22
Blowing Rock, North Carolina, 23
Blue Ball, Pennsylvania, 24
Boca Raton, Florida, 25
Bolivia, 117
Boone, Daniel, 129

Borden, Lizzie, 121
Boring, Oregon, 26
Bowlegs, Oklahoma, 27
Broadbottom, England, 28
Brown Willy, England, 29
Bugtussle, Kentucky, 30
Bush, George, 31
Bush, Kentucky, 31
Busti, New York, 32
Butternuts, New York, 33
Buttzville, New Jersey, 34

-C-
California, 44, 136, 146, 189,
  196, 197, 201
Canada, 97, 127, 168, 185
Catbrain, England, 35
Christmas, Michigan, 36
Clark, Marion, 162
Clark, Texas, 64
Climax, North Carolina, 37
Clowne, England, 38
Cockburn, Australia, 39
Cockermouth, England, 40
Cockroach Bay, Florida, 41
Colorado, 49, 96, 147
Come by Chance, Australia, 42
Conception, Missouri, 43
Connecticut, 131
Convict Lake, California, 44
Cooley, C.E., 162

Coral Sea Islands, 85
Cow Chip championship, 12
Cowlic, Arizona, 45
Coxsackie, New York, 46
Crackpot, England, 47
Crapo, Maryland, 48
Crook, Colorado, 49
Crook, George, 49
Cumming, Georgia, 50
Cunter, Switzerland, 51
Cut and Shoot, Texas, 52

-D-
Dead Horse Point State Park, 53
Dead Women Crossing, Okla-
  homa, 54
Denmark, 132
Devil's Dyke, England, 55
Devil's Tramping Ground, North
  Carolina, 56
Dick Peaks, Antarctica, 57
Dickshooter, Idaho, 58
Dikshit, India, 59
Dildo, Newfoundland, 60
Dillon, South Carolina, 165
Ding Dong, Texas, 61
Disappointment Creek, Alaska,
  62
Disappointment Islands, French
  Polynesia, 63
Dish, Texas, 64